The World War II
Warplane Guide

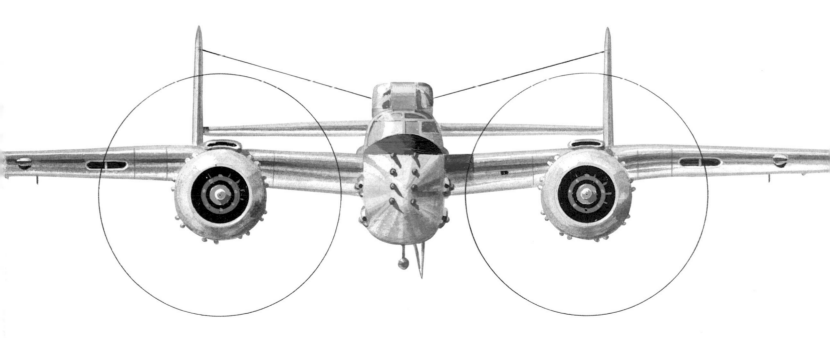

The World War II Warplane Guide

Charles Catton

CHARTWELL
BOOKS, INC.

Published by
CHARTWELL BOOKS, INC.
A Division of **BOOK SALES, INC.**
114 Northfield Avenue
Edison, New Jersey 08837

ISBN 0-7858-1328-4

Editorial and design by
Amber Books Ltd
Bradley's Close
74-77 White Lion Street
London N1 9PF

Project Editor: Naomi Waters
Design: Brian Rust

Artworks courtesy of Orbis Publishing Ltd and Aerospace Publishing Ltd

Printed in The Czech Republic

Contents

Junkers Ju 87 Stuka

Specification for D-1

Country of origin:	Germany
Powerplant:	One 1044kW (1400hp) Junkers Jumo 211J-1 inline piston engine
Armament:	Two 7.92mm (0.31in) MG 17 machine-guns in the wings, twin 7.92mm (0.31in) MG 81 machine-guns in the rear cockpit, plus 1800kg (3968lb) bombload
Weight:	3900kg (8598lbs) empty; 6600kg (14,550lbs) maximum
Dimensions:	13.8m (45ft 3in) span; 11.5m (37ft 9in) length; 3.9m (12ft 10in) height; 31.90m² (343.38sq ft) wing area
Performance:	410km/h (255mph) at 3840m (12,600ft); 7290m (23,915ft) ceiling
Flight range:	1535km (954 miles)
Crew:	One

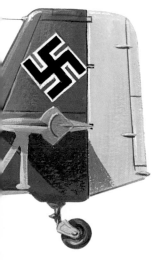

Known as the 'Stuka' (an abbreviation of *Sturzkampfflugzeug*), the Junkers Ju 87 will be forever linked with the Nazi blitzkrieg. Seemingly invincible when it first came to the world's attention with the invasion of Poland – and later those of France and the Low Countries – this myth was to be shattered by its dreadful losses in the Battle of Britain. Nonetheless, the type continued to give sterling service for the Luftwaffe on the Eastern Front, becoming a potent anti-tank weapon (as long as there were no fighters to oppose it).

Like the Messerschmitt Bf 109, the Stuka's prototype first flew with a Rolls-Royce Kestrel engine, but the first production A-series aircraft were equipped with the Junkers Jumo 210Ca. Three aircraft were sent to serve with the Condor Legion in the Spanish Civil War, and performed with distinction. By 1939, however, the new B-series became available, powered by the 895kW (1200hp) Jumo 211Da engine, which almost doubled the power available to the aircraft. It also introduced an automatic dive control, which would pull the aircraft out of a dive at a pre-set height. The pilot would operate the dive-brakes to begin the dive, line up the target, and, after the release of his bombload, push the button on top of his control stick to begin the pullout. Sirens were often used to add to the enemy's terror. The bombload was normally a 500kg (1102lb) bomb under the centreline, with four 50kg (110lb) bombs added under the wings if they operated within a short range of the target.

The B-2 variant could carry a 1000kg (2205lb) bomb at the expense of the rear gunner/navigator. The C-0 was built with folding wings and arrester hooks to serve aboard the unfinished *Graf Zeppelin* carrier. The Ju 87R was an extended-range Stuka, with extra tanks in the wings and provision for drop tanks. The next major version of the Ju 87 was the D-series, in service from late 1941, despite the Luftwaffe having recognized the vulnerability and increasing obsolescence of the aircraft. Powered by the 1044kW (1400hp) Jumo 211J-1 engine driving a broad-blade propeller, the Stuka could now carry much heavier loads: maximum bombload rose to 1800kg (3968lbs). The type's angular lines were cleaned up, but a silk purse could not be made from this sow's ear.

The D-3 was the most numerous of the D-series, featuring increased crew protection, a reflection of the by then common use of the Stuka as a close-support aircraft. Dive brakes were omitted on the D-7 and D-8 aircraft, the latter the last version in production when non-fighter production was terminated in late 1944. The other variants, the Ju 87G- and H-series, were conversions of D-series aircraft. The G was a specialized anti-armour version, mounting two 37mm (1.5in) guns under the wings. Flying a G-1, Hans-Ulrich Rudel was credited with destroying 519 Russian armoured vehicles. The Ju 87H was a dual-control trainer, made necessary by the specialist skills now needed to operate the Ju 87 over the front line.

Heinkel He 111H-20/R3

First flown on 25 February 1935, the Heinkel He 111 was designed by the brothers Siegfried and Walther Gunter as an airliner that would be easy to convert to a bomber, at a later date, for the nascent Luftwaffe. The prototypes, based heavily on the single-engined He 70 Blitz that had just entered Lufthansa service, proved to have a performance that exceeded that of most contemporary fighters. However, this was before the aircraft were equipped for the military role, and the first of the He 111A-0 series (10 in total) were so lacking in performance when carrying a bombload that they were soon sold to China. The first successful bomber conversion was the He 111B-1 series, which entered service in 1937. Powered by two Daimler-Benz DB600A engines, the aircraft had a top speed of 360km/h (224mph). Thirty He 111B-1s saw service in Spain during the Civil War, equipping K/88 of the pro-Republican Condor Legion. The next major variant put into service by the Luftwaffe was the He 111E, of which approximately 200 were built in 1938, all powered by the Junkers Jumo 211A-1 engine, which developed 746kW (950hp). As a result, the He 111E could lift a bombload of 2000kg (4409lbs).

A new planform wing with straight leading and trailing edges was adopted for the He 111F series aircraft, a move that was intended to simplify production. Twenty-four of these aircraft, carrying two Jumo 211A-3 engines, were sold to Turkey, the rest entering Luftwaffe service as the F-4. In 1939, the He 111J torpedo-bomber version was delivered to KGr 806, but all these aircraft were actually used as conventional bombers.

The 'classic' He 111, with its extensive nose glazing, was born with the He 111P, which first came into service with KG 157 in April 1939. Featuring a windscreen with a hinged section to aid the pilot during landing, the He 111P-series had its nose gun offset to port. Although intended as a stopgap, it remained in service after war broke out in September 1939.

By the time of the invasion of Poland, 400 examples of the He 111H series were in Luftwaffe service, and many of them saw service over Warsaw. Sent to the West in time for the invasion of France, He 111Hs were to feature heavily in the Battle of Britain. Over the course of the summer, 246 of the approximately 500 He 111Hs that began the battle were shot down. Despite this, the He 111 was far quicker than the Dornier Do 17, for example, and capable of absorbing heavy punishment from the RAF's fighters.

Although the Battle of Britain was perhaps the He 111's finest hour, the He 111H continued to be used and developed over the course of the war. The most widely used version, the H-6, could carry two 765kg (1687lb) torpedoes, and was armed with six 7.9mm (0.31in) MG 15 machine-guns and a forward-firing, 20mm (0.79in) cannon. The version shown here, the He 111H20/R3, carried a 2000kg (4410lb) bombload, and was largely used for night attacks on the Eastern Front. By the later years of the war, however, the He 111s in Luftwaffe service were either used as transports, or as the basis for the Reich's ever more colourful experiments with so-called 'wonder weapons'.

Specification

Country of origin:	Germany
Powerplant:	Two 1006kW (1350hp) Junkers Jumo 211F-2 in-line piston engines
Armament:	Three 13mm (0.51in) MG 131, four 7.92mm (0.303in) MG 81 machine-guns, plus up to 2000kg (4410lb) bombload
Weight:	8680kg (19,136lbs) empty; 14,000kg (30,865lbs) loaded
Dimensions:	22.6m (74ft 2in) span; 16.4m (53ft 10in) length; 4m (13ft 2in) height; 86.5m² (931.1sq ft) wing area
Performance:	435km/h (270mph) at 6000m (19,685ft); 8500m (27,890ft) ceiling
Flight range:	2059km (1280 miles)
Crew:	Five

Dornier Do 17P-1

Specification

Country of origin: Germany

Powerplant: Two 648kW (865hp) BMW 132N 9-cylinder radial piston engines

Armament: Three 7.9mm (0.31in) MG 15 machine-guns

Weight: 5625kg (12,400lbs) empty; 7660kg (16,887lbs) loaded

Dimensions: 18m (59ft 1in) span; 15.79m (52ft 10in) length; 4.56m (14ft 11in) height; 55m² (592sq ft) wing area

Performance: 396km/h (246mph) at 3999m (13,120ft); 6200m (20,340ft) ceiling

Flight range: 2248km (1367 miles)

Crew: Three

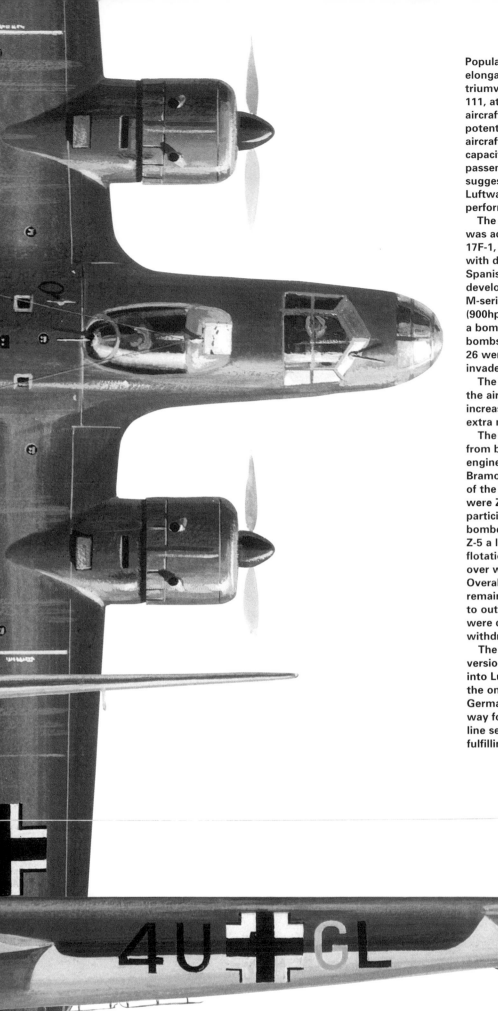

Popularly known as the 'Flying Pencil' due to its thin, elongated fuselage, the Dornier Do 17 was one of the triumvirate of Nazi bombers, along with the Ju 88 and He 111, at the outbreak of World War II. In an age when most aircraft designed in Germany had a secret military potential, the Do 17 was genuinely designed as a civil aircraft. It was intended to be a fast mailplane, with the capacity to carry six passengers. Lufthansa found the passenger accommodation cramped, but a test pilot suggested it might have potential as a bomber, and the Luftwaffe quickly adopted it on the basis of its performance.

The first production version was the Do 17E-1, which was accompanied into service by the almost identical Do 17F-1, the reconnaissance version. Both variants served with distinction with the Condor Legion during the Spanish Civil War. The Do 17M- and P-series were developed in tandem as direct replacements, although the M-series bomber variant had better engines, the 675kW (900hp) Bramo 323A-1 air-cooled radial. Both versions had a bomb-bay that could carry up to 1000kg (2205lbs) of bombs. Some Do 17Ms were exported to Yugoslavia, and 26 were destroyed on the ground when the Germans invaded in 1941.

The Do 17U-1 was a specialized pathfinder version of the aircraft, and only 12 were made. The cockpit had an increased height, and a five-man crew was carried, the extra man being another radio operator.

The final bomber version, the Do 17Z, initially suffered from being underpowered, using the same Bramo 323A-1 engines, but the Z-2 introduced the 746kW (1000hp) Bramo 323P engines with two-speed superchargers. Most of the Do 17 bombers involved in the Battle of Britain were Z-series aircraft, although a handful of E-series participated. The Z-3 was a dual-role, reconnaissance bomber, whilst the Z-4 was a dual-control trainer, and the Z-5 a long-range, reconnaissance aircraft, equipped with flotation bags and extra survival equipment for operations over water. Production of the Z-series ended in 1940. Overall, however, throughout its service life, the Do 17 remained under-gunned defensively, and could only hope to outrun its attackers. A small number of Z-series aircraft were converted to night-fighters, but they were withdrawn by early 1942.

The Do 215 was a designation applied to export versions of the Z-series aircraft, that were later brought into Luftwaffe service. Primarily reconnaissance aircraft, the only other variant of note was the Do 215B-5, the first German aircraft to carry the Lichtenstein radar, paving the way for the Me 110 and Ju 88. All Do 215s had left front-line service by mid-1942, spending the rest of the war fulfilling second-line duties.

Messerschmitt Bf 109E-3

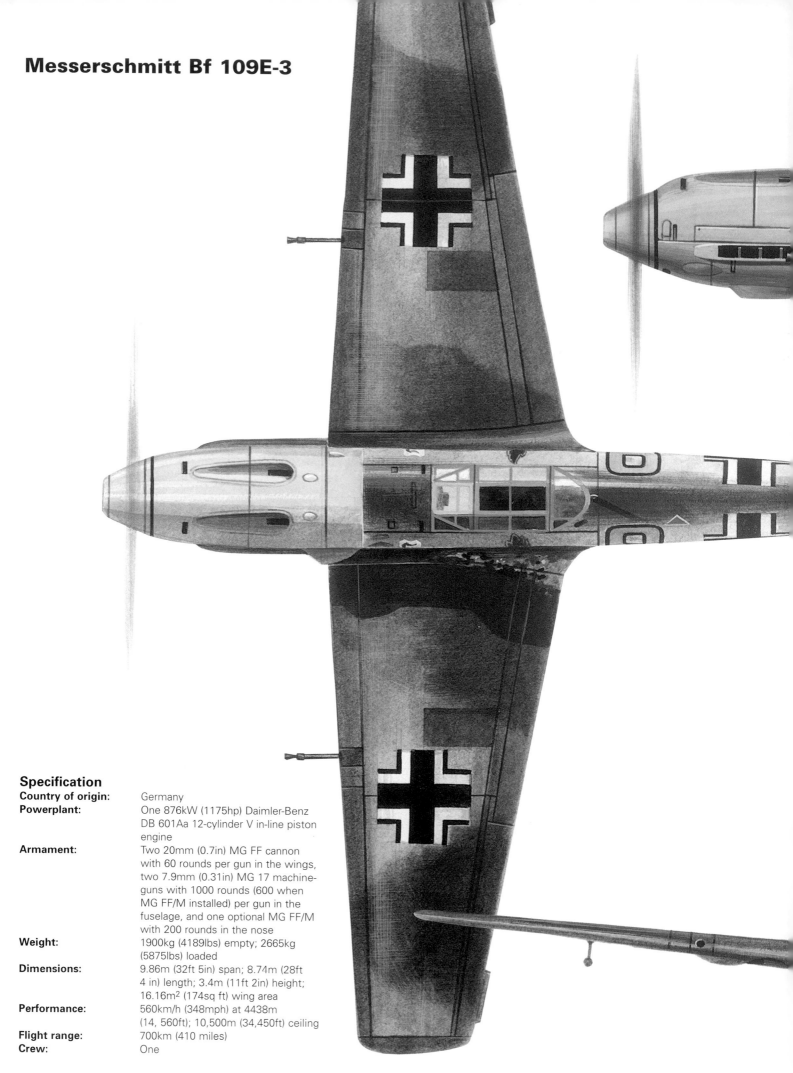

Specification

Country of origin:	Germany
Powerplant:	One 876kW (1175hp) Daimler-Benz DB 601Aa 12-cylinder V in-line piston engine
Armament:	Two 20mm (0.7in) MG FF cannon with 60 rounds per gun in the wings, two 7.9mm (0.31in) MG 17 machine-guns with 1000 rounds (600 when MG FF/M installed) per gun in the fuselage, and one optional MG FF/M with 200 rounds in the nose
Weight:	1900kg (4189lbs) empty; 2665kg (5875lbs) loaded
Dimensions:	9.86m (32ft 5in) span; 8.74m (28ft 4 in) length; 3.4m (11ft 2in) height; 16.16m² (174sq ft) wing area
Performance:	560km/h (348mph) at 4438m (14, 560ft); 10,500m (34,450ft) ceiling
Flight range:	700km (410 miles)
Crew:	One

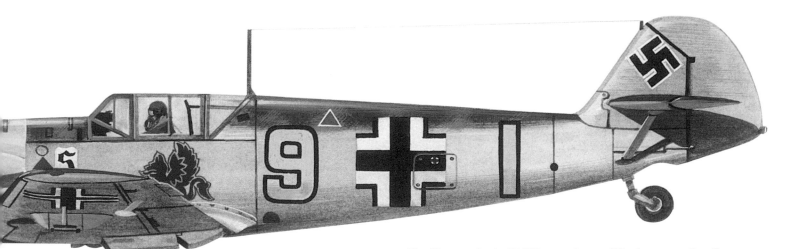

The Messerschmitt Bf 109 scored more kills than any other German aircraft during World War II. If it was later eclipsed by the Focke-Wulf Fw 190, it remained the backbone of the Luftwaffe's fighter arm. Although much changed from its original form, the final Bf 109K-14 was still recognizably the same aircraft as the V1 prototype rolled out in September 1935. Ironically, the prototype was powered by a Rolls-Royce Kestrel VI engine; it sufficiently impressed the German Air Ministry to win an order for 10 pre-production aircraft. Like most of its contemporaries, the Bf 109 went to Spain in the service of the Condor Legion, where it performed with distinction against the Republican aircraft.

By the outbreak of war in 1939, the Bf 109D was already giving way to the 'classic' Bf 109E that would feature so prominently in the Battle of Britain. The E-1 was able to outperform all opponents in the first eight months of the war. A subvariant, the E-1/B, was a fighter-bomber version, capable of carrying a 250kg (551lb) bomb. By 1940, production of the 'Emil' had reached 1868 aircraft. The E-2 and E-3 had two MG 17s in the nose, and two in the wings, with an MG FF/M firing through the nose. The E-4 had two nose MG 17s, and two MG FF/Ms in its wings. All these saw extensive use against the Allies in 1940; the experienced German flyers exacted a fearful toll on the untried British and French pilots. Nonetheless, as Allied tactics improved, German losses mounted. The Bf 109E-4/B, a fighter-bomber variant, proved difficult to intercept due to its high speed; a notable success was the sinking of HMS *Fiji* in 1941.

The Bf 109F smoothed off the Emil's angular lines, and introduced a 895kW (1200hp) Daimler-Benz DB 601E powerplant, with a revised armament of two MG 17s above the nose and the high-velocity MG 151 firing through the propeller, thereby reducing the amount of firepower available to the pilot. The F-3, the main version of the F-series introduced early 1942, had better handling and a top speed of 628km/h (390mph). A fighter-bomber variant, the F-4/B, could carry up to 500kg (1102lbs) of ordnance.

The most numerous variant, the G-series, entered service towards the end of 1942, sacrificing handling and manoeuvrability for outright performance. The fastest was the G-10, powered by the DB 605D engine, giving a top speed of 690km/h (429mph) with water injection, but large numbers of other subvariants were built.

The last two variants of this classic to see service in the war were the abortive, high-altitude H-series fighter, and the K-series aircraft, the last of which was the K-14.

Messerschmitt Bf 110

Specification for 110C-4

Country of origin:	Germany
Powerplant:	Two 821kW (1100hp) Daimler Benz DB 601A 12-cylinder V in-line piston engines
Armament:	Two 20mm (0.79in) MG 151 cannon and four 7.92mm (0.31in) MG 17 machine-guns in the nose, with one 7.92mm (0.31in) MG 812 twin gun facing aft, and provision for two 250kg (551lb) bombs under the fuselage
Weight:	5200kg (11,454lbs) empty; 6750kg (14,881lbs) loaded
Dimensions:	16.27m (5ft 3in) span; 12.65m (41ft 6in) length; 3.5m (11ft 6in) height; 38.4m² (413.3sq ft) wing area
Performance:	560km/h (349mph) at 7000m (22,965ft); 10,000m (32,810ft) ceiling
Flight range:	775km (482 miles)
Crew:	Two

First flown on 12 May 1936, the Messerschmitt Bf 110 was an attempt to produce a long-ranged fighter capable of holding its own with single-seat opponents. Impressed by the prototype, Göring ordered that production should proceed, and the first production aircraft emerged in the summer of 1938. Equipped with two 20mm (0.79in) MG FF cannon and four 7.92mm (0.31in) machine-guns, the Bf 110B-1 had a top speed of 455km/h (283mph). By the following year, however, the C-1 had entered service, powered by two 820kW (1100hp) Daimler-Benz DB 601A-1 engines. After the invasion of Poland, the type proved capable of shooting down the Polish fighters, but only on its own terms; it was not suited to a turning dogfight.

It was the lack of manoeuvrability that led to the type's failure in the Battle of Britain. The RAF's lighter Spitfire and Hurricane fighters could easily out-turn it at low speeds, and it was shot down in large numbers when forced to escort the Luftwaffe's bombers.

Operations after the invasion of Russia saw a similar pattern emerge, and although the E-, F- and G-series aircraft continued to serve on the front line, they did so in reduced numbers after 1942. By late 1943, the Bf 110s had found a new role as bomber-destroyer, armed with a motley collection of weapons, ranging from 20mm (0.79in) cannon to rocket mortars. They took a heavy toll of the USAAF B-17s and B-24s until the introduction of P-47s with drop tanks, prompting an even greater casualty rate amongst the Bf 110s. Thereafter, the type would only be found operating where Allied fighters were not likely to be found.

The Bf 110 undoubtedly found its *métier* as a night-fighter. First used in this role at the end of July 1940, the first sorties saw the twin-engined fighter guided to its prey by the cumbersome Himmelbett system, which used ground-based radar to co-ordinate attacks. Bf 110E-1/U-1s were the first variant to carry the Lichtenstein radar in 1941, but front-line units only received an updated version of the radar in mid-1942.

By this time the standard night-fighter variant was the F-4, powered by DB 601F-1 engines, and carrying four MG 17 machine-guns and two MG 151 cannon. Its only drawback was its limited range, which meant that it had to be in the right area at the right time to have a chance of intercepting Allied bombers. The definitive night-fighter was the Bf 110G-4, equipped with an uprated radar and, later, *schräge Musik* upward-firing cannon. From late 1943 to mid-1944, the G-4 formed the backbone of the Luftwaffe's night-fighting arm, but as the war moved into its final stages, it was superseded by the longer-ranged and better-performing Ju 88.

Junkers Ju 88

Perhaps the definitive German aircraft of World War II (though there are many to choose from), the Ju 88 was the Luftwaffe's 'jack-of-all-trades', serving in a wide variety of roles. Born out of a 1935 Luftwaffe requirement for a bomber capable of 500km/h (311mph), and carrying a bombload of up to 800kg (1765lbs), the first prototype was flown on 21 December 1936. Development was a slow process, and the first production Ju 88A-1s only reached the Luftwaffe in August 1939. Their first major mission was against the British Home Fleet, which only avoided serious damage because the bombs failed to explode. Despite this unpromising start, the Luftwaffe realized it had an aircraft with great potential. More than half of the Ju 88's total production were A-series variants, which were later used in a range of roles, including training, glider towing, freight and passenger transport. The next major variant was the C-series, developed as a night-fighter to counter the RAF's raids, and updated as the war progressed with Lichtenstein radar and *schräge Musik* upward firing cannon – usually two 20mm MG 151s.

The Ju 88D was a four-seat, long-range, reconnaissance aircraft, which, unlike the C-series, retained the glazed nose of the A-series. The G-series, which emerged in 1943, were designed as replacements for the C-series as night-fighters, but luckily for the RAF were only available in large numbers from mid-1944. They were usually armed with four ventral MG 151s and two *schräge Musik* guns. Reconnaissance was the role of the stretched H-series, apart from the H-2, which had an armament of no less than six MG 151s, for use against ships or aircraft in the Atlantic.

Only a few of the P-series anti-tank variant were made. The P-1 mounted a hand-loaded, 7.5cm (2.9in) Pak 40, whilst the P-2 and -3 had twin, 3.7cm (1.5in) anti-tank guns in a large gondola. The S-series, on the other hand, was an attempt to return the Ju 88 to its roots, and produce a fast bomber that stood a reasonable chance of returning from a raid. The maximum speed reached by the S-series was about 612km/h (380mph), which was some way behind contemporary fighters, and not as fast as the G-series night-fighters. A handful of the equivalent T-series reconnaissance aircraft were built.

Over its lifetime in World War II, the Ju 88 had been used as a bomber, dive-bomber, escort, night-fighter, tank-buster, anti-shipping aircraft, anti-submarine aircraft, glider-tug, supply aircraft, training aircraft, transport aircraft, close support, and torpedo-bomber. However, by the end of the conflict, the Ju 88 found perhaps its strangest role, as an unguided, pilotless missile in the Mistel experiment. Packed with explosives, and guided to their target by a fighter strapped to their back, the old Ju 88s performed one last time in the service of the Reich. Unfortunately for the German cause, most missed their targets. Despite this undignified end for some of these aircraft, the Ju 88 was one of the finest aeroplanes of the war.

Specification

Country of origin:	Germany
Powerplant:	Two 895kW (1200hp) Junkers Jumo 211B-1 12-cylinder inverted-V in-line piston engines
Armament:	Up to four 7.9mm (0.31in) MG 15 machine-guns, and up to 2250kg (4960lb) bombload
Weight:	7257kg (16,000lbs) empty; 10,705kg (23,600lbs) loaded
Dimensions:	18.4m (60ft 3in) span; 14.35m (47ft 1 in) length; 5.33m (17ft 6in) height; 54.5m² (586.63sq ft) wing area
Performance:	450km/h (280mph) at 5500m (18,050ft); 8000m (26,250ft) ceiling
Flight range:	1698km (1055 miles) with fuel in the forward bomb-bay
Crew:	Four

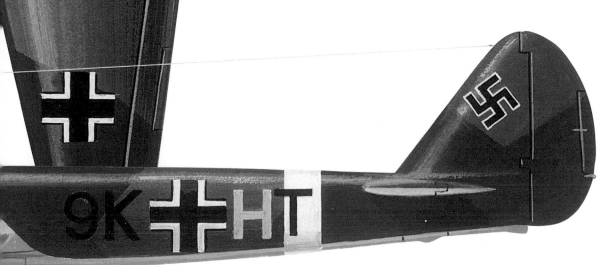

Focke-Wulf Fw 190D-9

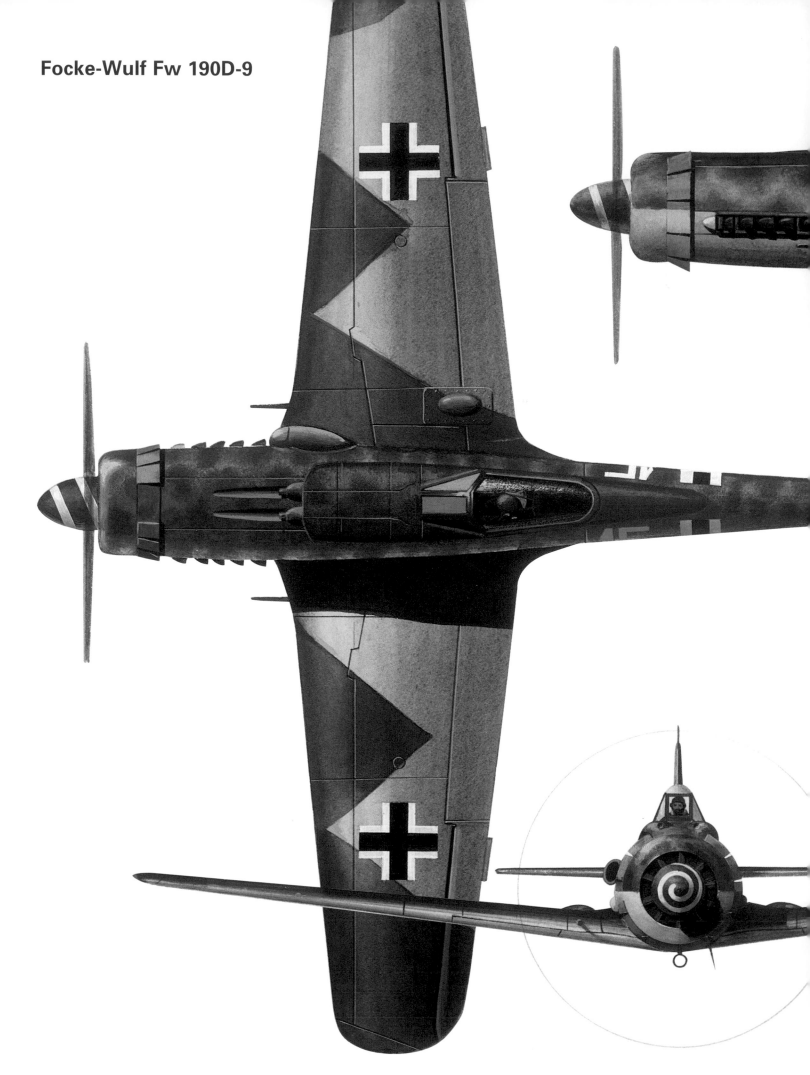

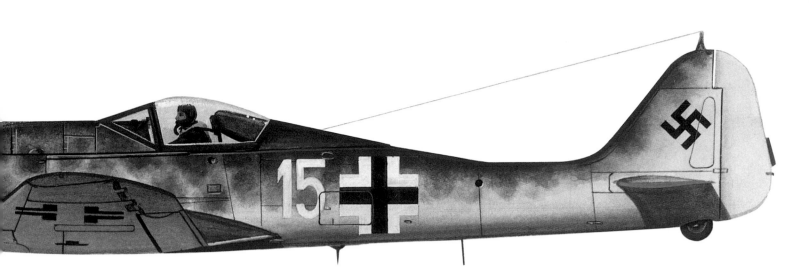

Along with the Messerschmitt Me 109, one of the great German fighter designs of World War II, the Focke-Wulf Fw 190 was destined to supplant its predecessor in the Luftwaffe's affections; so much so that by the end of the war over 20,000 examples had been built. The design was put forward in 1937 with two alternative powerplants: the Daimler-Benz DB 601 in-line, and the BMW 139 radial. In what appeared to be a retroactive step, the radial version was chosen, as it was thought that it would have greater development potential, and the prototype first flew in June 1939. By 1940, service trials of the Fw 190A-0, powered by the new BMW 801 14-cylinder radial, were under way at the Luftwaffe's testing ground at Rechlin. The first major type to enter service was the Fw 190A-1 with the 1194kW (1600hp) BMW 801C engine installed, with 100 examples delivered to the Luftwaffe by May 1941. However, while pilots liked the aircraft's handling and performance, which was far better than the RAF's contemporary Spitfire V, they criticized the type's light armament – only four 7.9mm (0.31in) machine-guns. This was corrected in the A-2 model, which carried two 20mm (0.8in) MG FF cannon in the wing roots, combined with two MG 17 machine-guns, at the cost of a slight reduction in top speed to 614km/h (382mph).

The A-3 variant introduced in early 1942 continued this trend, adding another two cannon, but also receiving an uprated engine, the 1269kW (1700hp) BMW 801DG. A bomb-carrying version, the A3/U1, also appeared at this time. The A-4, entering service over the summer, had a top speed of 670km/h (416mph) thanks to its water-injected, 1567kW (2100hp) BMW 801D-2 engine. The RAF's Spitfire IX and newly introduced Typhoon seemed to be no match, and 92 RAF fighters were lost during the Dieppe operation. Increasingly, the Fw 190 was used as a fighter-bomber, capable of carrying bombs, rockets and even torpedoes (the Fw 190A-5/U-15 variant), although it was still inflicting a huge toll on the Allied bombing effort as an interceptor.

Neither the Fw 190 B- or C-series was a great success, but the D-series, particularly the D-9, powered by the 1323kW (1776hp) Junkers Jumo 213A-1 in-line engine, was the best German production fighter aircraft of the war. The 'Dora-Nine' was armed with two 20mm (0.8in) MG 151 cannon and two 13mm (0.5in) MG 131 machine-guns, more than a match for the P-51 Mustang. Introduced in August 1944, it was hamstrung in the effort to regain air superiority by Germany's lack of fuel and pilots. The F- and G-series were dedicated ground-attack aircraft. The last 'version' was the Ta 152, derived from the Fw 190 by the designer Kurt Tank, and optimized for high-altitude interception.

Specification

Country of origin:	Germany
Powerplant:	One 1669kW (2240hp) Junkers Jumo 213A-1 in-line piston engine with MW-50 methanol-water injection
Armament:	Two 20mm Mauser MG 151/20 cannon with 250 rounds per gun, and two 13mm (0.51mm) Rheinmetall Borsig MG 131 machine-guns, with 475 rounds per gun
Weight:	3490kg (7694lbs) empty; 4840kg (10,670lbs) loaded
Dimensions:	10.5m (34ft 5in) span; 10.21m (33ft 5in) length; 3.36m (11ft) height; 18.3m² (196.98sq ft) wing area
Performance:	686km (426mph) at 7000m (21,650ft); 11,278m (37,000ft) ceiling; 7 minutes 6 seconds to 6000m (19,685ft) climb
Flight range:	837km (520 miles)
Crew:	One

Messerschmitt Me 163

Specification

Country of origin:	Germany
Powerplant:	One Walther HWK 509A-1 rocket motor with a high-altitude thrust of 16.67kN (3748lb)
Armament:	Two 30mm Rheinmetall MK 108 cannon, with 60 rounds per gun
Weight:	1900kg (4190lbs) empty; 4310kg (9502lbs) loaded
Dimensions:	9.4m (30ft 7in) span; 5.85m (19ft 2in) length; 2.76m (9ft) height; 18.5m² (199sq ft) wing area
Performance:	960km/h (597mph) above 3000m (9845ft); 12,000m (39,370ft) ceiling
Flight range:	130km (80 miles)
Crew:	One

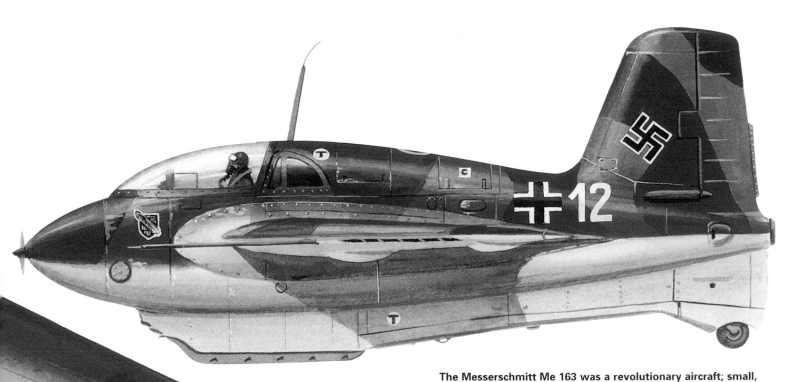

The Messerschmitt Me 163 was a revolutionary aircraft; small, agile and nearly twice as fast as its opponents, it struck real fear into the Allies before its limitations were realized. Its roots lay in a request by the German Air Ministry for Dr Alexander Lippisch to design an airframe to hold the Walter I-203 rocket engine. Although that project came to nothing, Dr Lippisch joined Messerschmitt in 1939, and was given his own team to work on rocket experiments. In 1940, he took an all-wood DFS 194 glider powered by a I-203 to Peenemünde, where it achieved speeds of up to 547km/h (340mph) and astonishing rates of climb. This ignited interest in the project, and six prototypes designated the Me 163A were to be tested with the uprated I-203b, rated at 7.36kN (1653lbs) of static thrust. Trials began in March 1941, but the first powered flight did not happen until 13 August that year. On 2 October, the test pilot, Heini Dittmar, was towed aloft before starting the motor. He suddenly lost control as the nose dipped violently, the first effects of approaching the sound barrier. His recorded speed of 1004 km/h (624mph) was 250km/h (155mph) above the official world-speed record.

The pre-production version, the Me 163B, was to be powered by the R II-211 motor. However, it had teething problems, as its two reactive components were extremely unstable, and testing twice resulted in an explosion that destroyed the entire building. The use of an unsprung take-off trolley and landing skid also made these actions potentially fatal for the pilot. However, production went ahead, with the aircraft allocated the name Komet. Although a test squadron was formed as early as the spring of 1943, the programme suffered a major delay as a result of the bombing of the Messerschmitt factory at Regensberg in August, and it was only by February 1944 that the first Me 163B 1a production aircraft began to arrive at Lechfeld.

The aircraft itself was a simple affair: a tail-less, winged glider powered by the Type 509A rocket motor, which could achieve 14.71kN (3307lb) static thrust at sea level. It was armed with two cannon, early versions carrying the 20mm (0.8in) MG 151, but most had the 30mm (1.17in) MK 108 with 60 rounds per gun. The first combat engagements were not a success, due to a combination of technical failures and high closing speeds. Two were lost to enemy fire before a single enemy aircraft was destroyed, but the first victory came on 24 August 1944, when four B-17s were shot down. The closing speed proved too fast for pilots to aim successfully, so a system was devised to use upward-firing guns triggered by photo-electric cells, but this was used only once before the war ended. In the final analysis, as a combat aircraft the Komet was a failure. Over 80 per cent of its losses occurred on landing or take-off, and only nine enemy bombers were claimed, although around 300 Me 163s were in front-line service.

Messerschmitt Me 262

Specification
Country of Origin: Germany
Powerplant: Two Junkers Jumo 004B-1 turbojets producing 8.83kN (1984lb) static thrust each
Armament: four 30mm Rheinmetall-Borsig MK 108A-3 cannon in the nose
Weight: 3795kg (8378lbs) empty; 6387kg (14,080lbs) loaded
Dimensions: 12.5m (40ft 11in) span; 10.58m (34ft 9in) length; 3.85m (12ft 7in) height; 21.73m2 (234sq ft) wing area
Performance: 827km/h (514mph) at sea level; 12,190+m (40,000+ft) ceiling
Flight range: 1050km (652 miles)
Crew: One

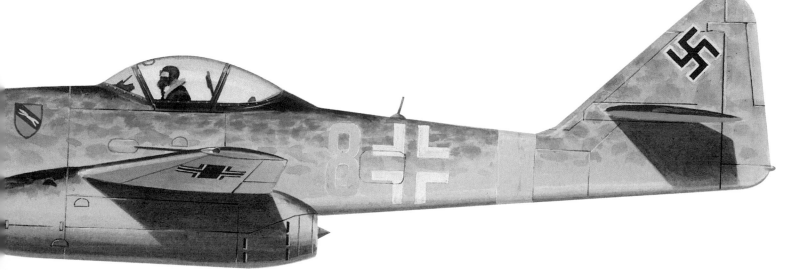

The first operational jet fighter, the Me 262 was born in January 1939, when Messerschmitt was ordered by the German Air Ministry to supply a design for a turbojet-powered fighter. As the engines available at the time lacked sufficient power, the design team opted for a twin-engined design. Although not the first jet fighter design – the Heinkel He 280 first flew in March 1941, followed later in the year by Frank Whittle's Gloster design in England – the Messerschmitt Me 262 would be the only one to achieve operational status. However, it would be a long wait for the Luftwaffe. The BMW 003 engines did not arrive until November 1941, and developed problems on the first flight. Replacement Jumo 004 engines were installed in the V3 prototype, and this first flew on 18 July 1942, performing beautifully. When Adolf Galland, the German ace, flew the V4 prototype in May 1943 he was won over by the aircraft – shortly afterwards a production order for 100 examples was issued. Its former rival, the Heinkel He 280, had been cancelled two months beforehand.

Unfortunately for the Luftwaffe, the US raid on the Messerschmitt factory at Regensburg in August 1943 destroyed the infant production lines, and the operation had to be moved to the Bavarian Alps, taking up precious time. Further time was to be wasted when Hitler became involved. Viewing the definitive V6 prototype in East Prussia in November 1943, he asked Messerschmitt to convert each aircraft built to carry bombs, a process that would delay each unit by a further two weeks. An experimental version was even fitted with a forward-facing 50mm cannon for anti-tank missions. Operations finally began with Ekdo 262 based at Lechfeld in the early summer of 1944, by which time the Allied air offensive had already gained the upper hand. A few examples were used in the reconnaissance role, but the first dedicated fighter squadron was not established until October 1944 – Kommando Nowotny, equipped with 30 Me 262A-1a variants powered by Jumo 004B-1 turbojets, and armed with four 30mm cannon. Although its top speed of 855km/h (531mph) meant that it could outrun any Allied aircraft, it was found to be vulnerable in its landing pattern, as the engines took a long time to spool up to full power. Allied fighters began to wait for Me 262s to return from their missions, and eventually the Luftwaffe had to provide conventional fighter cover to protect their precious jets. However there were never enough Me 262s available in sufficient numbers to dent the Allied bombing effort – even the use of the R4M unguided rocket in March 1945 had no effect. The aircraft was undoubtedly ahead of its time – it was far more advanced than anything the Allies possessed, and it kickstarted the post-war effort to break the sound barrier.

Arado Ar 234 Blitz

Specification

Country of origin: Germany

Powerplant: Two Junkers Jumo 004B-1 turbojets producing 8.83kN (1984lbs) static thrust each

Armament: Two fixed, aft-facing 20mm (0.8in) Mauser MG 151/20 cannon, with 200 rounds per gun

Weight: 5200kg (11,464lbs) empty; 9800kg (21,605lbs) loaded

Dimensions: 14.41m (46ft 3in) span; 12.64m (41ft 5in) length; 4.29m (14ft 1in) height; 26.4m² (284.16sq ft) wing area

Performance: 742km/h (461mph) at 6000m (19,685ft); 10,000m (32,810ft) ceiling

Flight range: 1556km (967 miles)

Crew: One

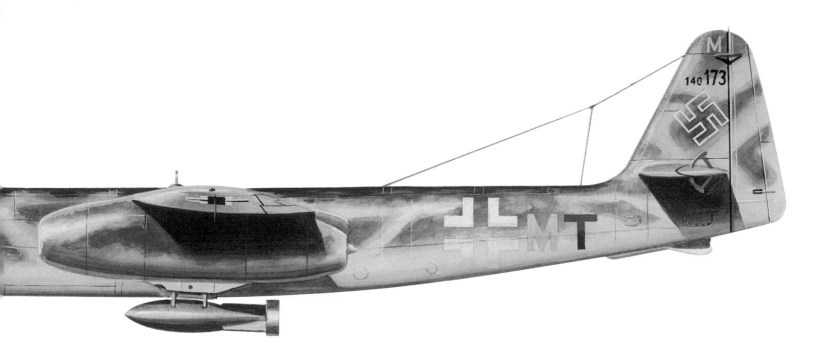

The first jet-bomber aircraft to enter service, the Arado Blitz, was the brainchild of engineers Walter Blume and Hans Rebeski. Apart from its turbojet nacelles, the design was very clean and conventional. Single-seat, with an entirely glazed nose section, the bulk of the all-metal fuselage contained fuel tanks in order to give the reconnaissance version a sufficient range to be useful. The most unconventional aspect was the landing gear, or lack of it. Deciding that there was no room for undercarriage gear, the first prototype took off from a detachable trolley, and landed on retractable skids. The handling problems this caused on the ground led to the idea being quickly abandoned after the prototype began flight trials in June 1943, and the production variant, the Ar 234B, was equipped with conventional landing gear (the space was gained by removing the central fuel tank, and enlarging the front and aft fuel tanks to compensate). The seven A-series prototypes were used to test pressurization, rocket-assisted take-off packs, the new Junkers 004B engine and even ejector seats.

The first B-series prototypes flew in early 1944, testing the RF 2C periscopic sight, racks for bombs or fuel tanks under the engine nacelles, and a centreline hardpoint for a bomb. Twenty pre-production B-0 aircraft were built, 13 of which went straight to the Luftwaffe testing centre at Rechlin; a small number of B-1 reconnaissance variants were then built. The standard production model was the Ar 234B-2, which could perform either bombing or reconnaissance missions. The B-2 had an unusual defensive armament of two fixed, rear-firing MG 151 cannon, sighted by the periscopic sight, although it could in practice outrun most Allied fighters unless caught near its airfield. All pilots who flew the aircraft praised its handling, and it was capable of manoeuvring hard if necessary. Engine failure was a common experience, as the early turbojets were not reliable and demanded constant maintenance.

When, by early October 1944, the Luftwaffe began to operate the Blitz in numbers, the Germans were able, once more, to gain good-quality information on Allied dispositions in north-west Europe, and even southern England. The Blitz was also used to support the Ardennes offensive in December 1944, and it was an Arado Ar 234B that finally destroyed the Ludendorff bridge over the Rhine in March 1945, after the Americans had captured it intact. In the same month, a few B-2s fitted with cannon in a ventral tray, and equipped with the FuG 218 Neptun radar, were active on night-fighting duties. However, operations stopped shortly afterwards, as the war came to a close.

The only other variant of note was the four-engined Ar 234C, which mounted Junkers Jumo 003As in paired nacelles, but which never fully entered production.

Consolidated PBY-5A

Specification

Country of origin: USA

Powerplant: Two 895kW (1200hp) Pratt & Whitney R-1830-92 Twin Wasp radial engines

Armament: Two 12.7mm (0.5in) and three 7.62mm (0.3in) Browning machine-guns, plus 1816kg (4000lb) bombload or four 295kg (650lb) depth charges or two Mark 13-2 torpedoes

Weight: 9485kg (20,910lbs) empty; 16,067kg (35,420lbs) loaded

Dimensions: 31.7m (104ft) span; 19.47m (63ft 11in) length; 6.15m (20ft 2in) height; 130m² (1400sq ft) wing area

Performance: 282km/h (175mph); 3690m (13,000ft) ceiling

Flight range: 3782km (2350 miles) loaded

Crew: Seven to nine

Testament to this aircraft's role in World War II is the fact that more of them were built than any other flying-boat or floatplane during the conflict, including several types such as the Martin PBM that were supposed to replace it. Born from a US Navy requirement issued in 1933, the Isaac M. Laddon design first flew in 1935, and was essentially a 'cleaned-up' version of the earlier Consolidated P2Y. A unique feature was the PBY's wingfloats, which could be electrically retracted to form the wing tips while in flight. The first examples were delivered in October 1936, by which time a further contract for 50 PBY-2s had been placed with Consolidated. The PBY-2 was equipped with four wing racks, capable of carrying up to 454kg (1000lb) loads each, and had 12.7mm (0.5in) machine-guns in the waist positions. The Navy was so pleased with its acquisition that yet another order for 66 PBY-3s was placed that November, the new variant being powered by 746kW (1000hp) R-1830-66 Twin Wasps. The PBY-4 followed in late 1937, introducing the characteristic 'bug-eye', waist-position blisters and uprated engines. One example so impressed the Soviets that they put it into licenced production, and over 1000 were used in World War II with Soviet weapons and Polikarpov engines.

The RAF was also extremely impressed by the PBY, and adopted it as the Catalina Mk 1 for Coastal Command. The name was later also adopted by the US Navy. The RAF's Mk 1 was essentially the same as the latest US variant, the PBY-5, which was also built under licence by Canadian Vickers and Boeing of Canada. The PBY-5A was an amphibious version of the PBY-5, whose undercarriage only had a minor effect on performance. The USAAF received 230 examples (designated OA-10A) for search-and-rescue missions, one of the Catalina's many roles. The RAF was the first to put a radar into the aircraft, mounting the ASV Mk II radar in the Catalina Mk IVA. It was an RAF Catalina that famously found the German battleship *Bismarck* in the Atlantic after it had eluded its pursuers, and enabled the British to finally sink her. In the Pacific, the US used all-black PBY-5As, or 'Black Cats' to track down Japanese ships with their on-board radar, and sink them with bombs, depth charges and fragmentation grenades.

One of the licenced production plants, the Naval Aircraft Factory at Philadelphia, produced an improved Catalina, which was designated the PBN-1, and named the Nomad. It had a redesigned hull, greater load-carrying wing, reshaped tail and increased armament, now sporting three or more 12.7mm (0.50in) machine-guns. Consolidated took this design and made it an amphibian equipped with a centrimetric radar in a teardrop-shaped pod above the cockpit, and twin 12.7mm (0.50in) guns in the bow turret. This final variant was designated the PBY-6A, which was also delivered to the RAF as the Catalina Mk VI, and to the USAAF as the OA-10B.

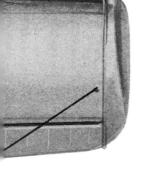

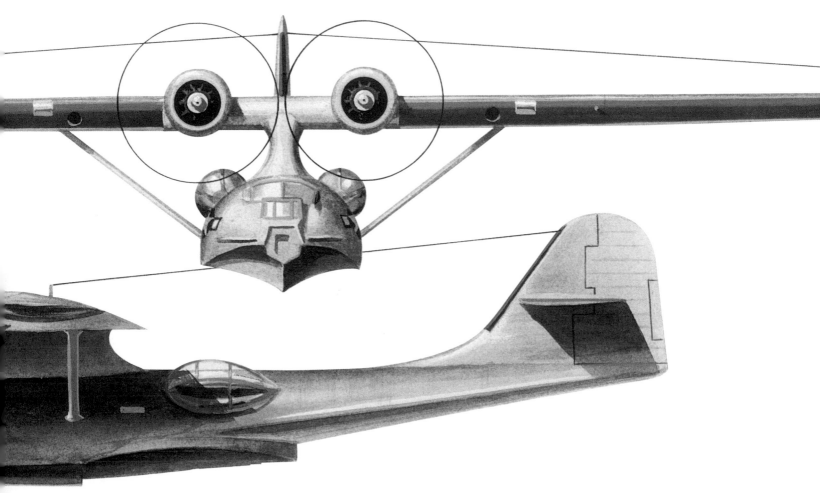

Boeing B-17G Flying Fortress

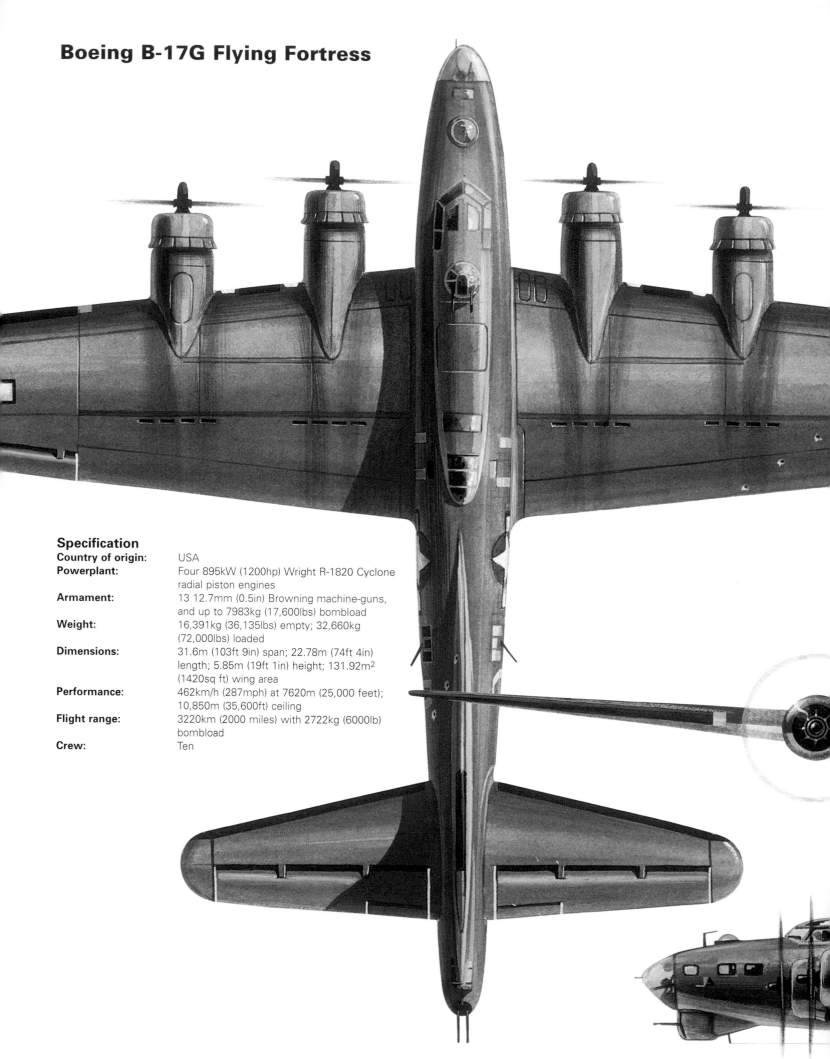

Specification

Country of origin: USA

Powerplant: Four 895kW (1200hp) Wright R-1820 Cyclone radial piston engines

Armament: 13 12.7mm (0.5in) Browning machine-guns, and up to 7983kg (17,600lbs) bombload

Weight: 16,391kg (36,135lbs) empty; 32,660kg (72,000lbs) loaded

Dimensions: 31.6m (103ft 9in) span; 22.78m (74ft 4in) length; 5.85m (19ft 1in) height; 131.92m² (1420sq ft) wing area

Performance: 462km/h (287mph) at 7620m (25,000 feet); 10,850m (35,600ft) ceiling

Flight range: 3220km (2000 miles) with 2722kg (6000lb) bombload

Crew: Ten

Famed for its role in the Allied bombing campaign over Germany, the Boeing B-17 will always be one of the most recognizable of World War II bombers. When in 1934 the US Army Air Corps put out a request for a multi-engined bomber, the Boeing design team decided to build the four-engined Model 299, which dwarfed its competition. The first flight on 28 July 1935 proved very successful, and Boeing registered the name 'Flying Fortress' for its new bomber. Despite a well-documented fatal crash of the prototype – due to human error – when it had US Army officials on board, the Air Corps was sufficiently impressed to order Y1B-17 prototypes. So opposed was the US Navy to an aircraft that it saw as taking over its appointed role as protector of the United States, that only 39 of the B-17B production model were built, despite the fact that it was the fastest and highest-flying bomber in the world at that time.

In 1939, a refined version, the B-17C, was ordered, equipped with self-sealing tanks, increased armour and defensive armament, and other extra equipment. Although heavier than the B-17B, the new 895kW (1200hp) engines actually made it faster, with a top speed of 515km/h (320mph). Twenty B-17Cs entered service with the RAF as the Fortress Mk 1, but the latter's inexperience of high-altitude flight meant that accidents occurred, and the type was relegated to Coastal Command. The B-17D, which was in service at the time of Pearl Harbor – some even arriving over the airfield at the same time as the Japanese attackers – proved not to be a great success in the Pacific. The differences between the B-17C and B-17D were largely internal.

The B-17E, which entered service in December 1941, was considerably different, however. It had a dorsal fin and larger tail to give the aircraft more stability, and carried 10 12.7mm (0.5in) machine-guns and two 7.62mm (0.3in) guns in the nose. This was the first variant in mass production, and 45 were supplied to the RAF as Fortress Mk IIAs. The B-17E, along with its successor, the B-17F (RAF Fortress Mk II), was to form the backbone of the US bombing effort from late 1942 to mid-1944. Again, the differences between the models were largely internal, the only visible change being the new, single-piece, Plexiglas nose.

Last of the major production variants, the B-17G (RAF Fortress Mk III) drew on the years of experience that the USAAF now had in operating over Germany. The most important change was the addition of a powered chin turret armed with twin 12.7mm (0.5in) machine-guns, which ended the Luftwaffe's favoured tactic of attacking B-17 formations frontally. Although the B-17G had improved turbochargers, its extra weight meant that its cruising speed fell to only 293km/h (182mph). The RAF's later Fortresses were largely used by Coastal Command. The next largest user of the B-17 was actually the Luftwaffe's KG 200, who used captured Fortresses for a number of clandestine missions.

Grumman F4F-4 Wildcat

Specification

Country of origin: USA

Powerplant: One 895kW (1200hp) Pratt & Whitney R-1830-36 Twin Wasp radial piston engine

Armament: Six 12.7mm (0.5in) Browning machine-guns, and two 45kg (100lb) bombs

Weight: 2612kg (5758lbs) empty; 3607kg (7952lbs) loaded

Dimensions: 11.58m (38ft) span; 8.76m (28ft 9in) length; 2.81m (9ft 3in) height; 24.15m² (260sq ft) wing span

Performance: 512km/h (318mph) at 5915m (19,400ft)

Flight range: 1239km (770 miles)

Crew: One

Although known as the Grumman Wildcat, the majority of these carrier fighters were not actually built by Grumman; many of those in foreign use were known as Martlets. Although its first combat victory was scored by a British pilot near Gibraltar in September 1941, the Wildcat will be remembered for its sterling work in defying the Japanese Zero fighters in the first half of the war in the Pacific. In 1936, the US Navy authorized the building of a biplane prototype fighter, the XF4F-1. It was then decided to build a monoplane, and a new prototype, the XF4F-2, was first flown on 2 September 1937. It was powered by a 783kW (1050hp) Pratt & Whitney R-1830-66 Twin Wasp Engine, and could attain a top speed of 467km/h (290mph). The US Navy decided not to put the aircraft into production, but returned it to Grumman asking for it to be developed further. The prototype was rebuilt as the XF4F-3, with an uprated Twin Wasp engine, and modifications to its wing and tail area, all of which resulted in a far better performance.

Although the US Navy now ordered 78 F4F-3 production aircraft, Grumman decided to offer the aircraft for export, and quantities were bought by both the French and Greek governments. By the time these aircraft were ready for delivery, however, both countries had fallen to the Germans, and the British agreed to purchase the aircraft. Christened the Martlet Mk 1, these first began to arrive in July 1940. Three other versions of the Wildcat served with the Fleet Air Arm, the folding-wing Mk II, 10 F4F-4As and the 30 Greek aircraft as the Mk III, and the Lend-Lease F4F-4Bs as the Mk IV. Most served on board small escort carriers, and were all renamed Wildcats in March 1944 as part of an initiative to standardize names.

The first US Wildcats flew in August 1940, followed by 95 F4F-3As powered by the R-1830-90 engine with supercharger in 1941. The F4F-4 included a number of improvements, such as increased armour, a six-gun armament, folding wings and self-sealing tanks, and entered service only a month before the attack on Pearl Harbor. Wildcats served with distinction in the battles of the Coral Sea and Midway, and were heavily involved in operations such as the landings at Guadalcanal until superseded in service in 1943. The final production variant of the Wildcat was the F4F-7 reconnaissance aircraft, which had increased fuel capacity at the expense of its armament. Only 21 examples were built.

From 1942, Grumman was concentrating on the F6F Hellcat, and licensed General Motors to continue production of the Hellcat as the FM-1, 312 of which went to the British as the Martlet Mk V. An improved version, the FM-2, was powered by a 1007kW (1350hp) Wright R-1820-56 Cyclone 9 engine, and had a larger tail. No less than 4777 examples were built, of which 370 went to the British as the Wildcat Mk VI.

Curtiss P-40
Warhawk/Kittyhawk

Specification for P-40N-20 Warhawk

Country of origin: USA

Powerplant: One 1015kW (1360hp) Allison V-1710-81 in-line piston engine

Armament: Six 12.7mm (0.5in) machine-guns, and one 227kg (500lb) bomb

Weight: 2724kg (6000lbs) empty; 4018kg (8850lbs) maximum

Dimensions: 11.42m (37ft 4in) span; 10.2m (33ft 4in) length; 3.77m (12ft 4in) height; 21.95m² (236sq ft) wing area

Performance: 609km/h (378mph) at 3210m (10,500ft); 11,630m (38,000ft) ceiling; 6 minutes 42 seconds to 4590m (15,000ft) climb

Flight range: 386km (240 miles)

Crew: One

At the time of the Japanese attack on Pearl Harbor, the P-40 was the USAAF's most numerous fighter. The type went on to serve in a wide variety of theatres in World War II, despite being outclassed by the latest Axis fighter designs, and later overshadowed by the three classic American fighters, the P-38, P-47 and P-51. First flown as the X17Y prototype, the design subsequently flew as the P-36 Hawk with a Pratt and Whitney radial engine, and, in October 1938, as the XP-40 fitted with the supercharged Allison V-1710 V12. As a result of its performance, it won substantial orders, and most of the P-40A production aircraft went to the RAF as the Tomahawk Mk I. All USAAF examples were known as Warhawks.

A modified version, with improved cockpit armour and two nose-mounted, 12.7mm (0.5in) and four wing-mounted, 7.62mm (0.3in) machine-guns was designated the P-40B, or Tomahawk MkIIA in the RAF, while the P-40C (Tomahawk Mk IIB) was fitted with self-sealing fuel tanks. When it arrived in the North African theatre in 1941, it was found to be far inferior to the Bf 109, and was thus relegated to a ground-attack role. The P-40D had a slightly shorter nose, in which the radiator had been moved forward and deepened, a sufficient change in appearance for the RAF to change its name to Kittyhawk. The first variant bought in large numbers by the USAAF was the P-40E, armed with six 12.7mm (0.5in) machine-guns in the wings, which was designated the Kittyhawk Mk IA in the RAF's service. The marriage of an American design to a British-designed engine, the Merlin, which was to work so well in the P-51 Mustang, was tried with the P-40F (Kittyhawk Mk II), which was equipped with the Packard licence-built engine.

The P-40K had an uprated Allison engine, which brought the type's performance close to that of the Bf 109E and Zero. Likewise, the P-40M had another improved Allison engine, with about 600 being delivered to the USAAF, and the L variant had an uprated, licence-built Merlin. The most numerous variant was the P-40N or Kittyhawk Mk IV, of which no less than 5219 were built. Powered by the 1015kW (1369hp) Allison V-1710-81 engine, it had racks for up to 680kg (1500lbs) of bombs, one of which was on the centreline. No less than 1000 of this variant were ordered for the USAAF, despite their increasing obsolescence, but production was cancelled in September 1944 when only 220 had been completed.

Although most USAAF P-40s served in the Pacific, examples were also to be found serving in the Mediterranean alongside those of the RAF and other Commonwealth countries. Several thousand were also supplied to the Soviet Union and China.

North American B-25J Mitchell

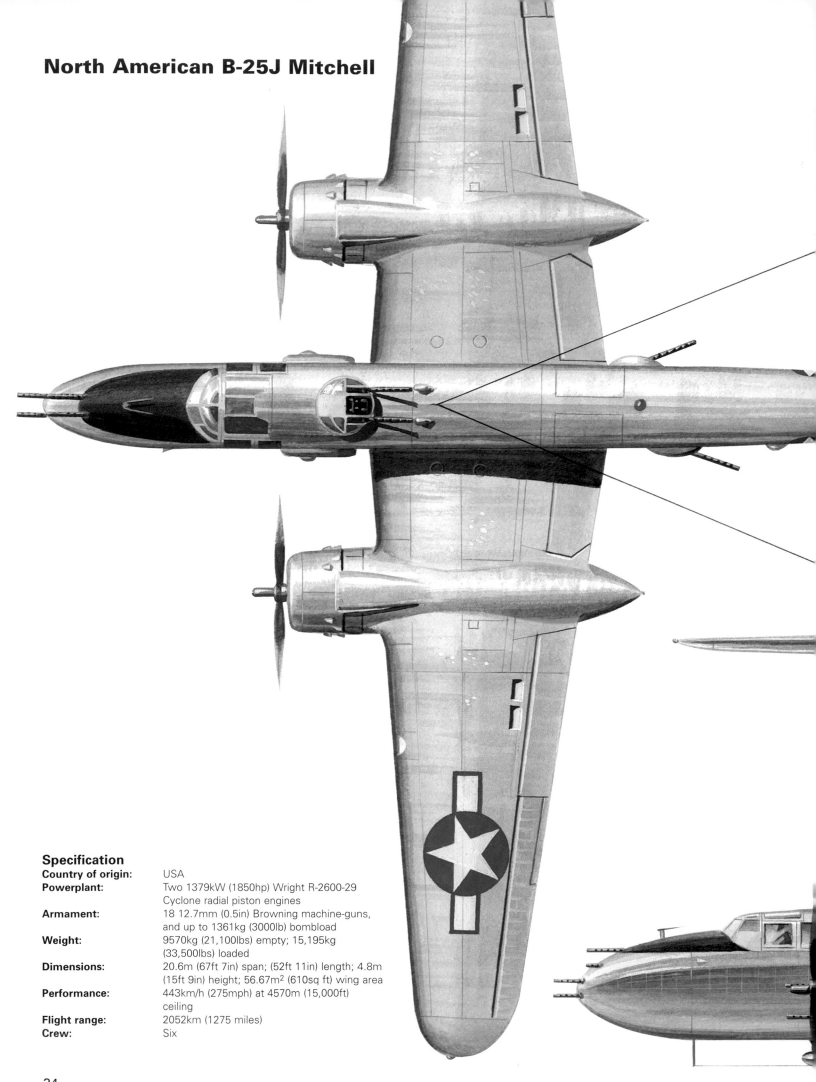

Specification

Country of origin: USA

Powerplant: Two 1379kW (1850hp) Wright R-2600-29 Cyclone radial piston engines

Armament: 18 12.7mm (0.5in) Browning machine-guns, and up to 1361kg (3000lb) bombload

Weight: 9570kg (21,100lbs) empty; 15,195kg (33,500lbs) loaded

Dimensions: 20.6m (67ft 7in) span; (52ft 11in) length; 4.8m (15ft 9in) height; 56.67m² (610sq ft) wing area

Performance: 443km/h (275mph) at 4570m (15,000ft) ceiling

Flight range: 2052km (1275 miles)

Crew: Six

The private venture NA-40 design was already being built when the US Army Air Corps issued a requirement for a medium bomber. First flown in January 1939, it was a twin-engined design with tricycle landing gear, and a second prototype, the NA-40B, flew only a few months later, with uprated engines. Although it was quickly written off in an accident, the NA-40B had impressed the USAAC pilots, and North American was asked to continue development with a number of changes: a widening of the fuselage to allow the bombload to be doubled, a redesign of the cockpit position, an increase in crew numbers to five, and a greater defensive armament of three 7.62mm (0.3in) machine-guns and one 12.7mm (0.5in) machine-gun. This new aircraft was designated the B-25, and by the time that it first flew in August 1939, North American had already received a contract for 184 examples.

Equipped with two 1268kW (1700hp) Pratt & Whitney R-2600-9 engines, at first the B-25 had difficulties due to a lack of directional stability, but this was cured by removing the dihedral (or slope) of the wings outboard of the engines. After only 24 examples, production shifted to the B-25A, which added extra armour for the pilots and self-sealing fuel tanks, and 40 of these were delivered before a new variant emerged, the B-25B, which was equipped with Bendix dorsal and ventral, twin-gun turrets, although its rear turret was removed. In April 1942, the B-25B came to the world's attention when it was used to bomb Tokyo for the first time. Launched from the deck of *USS Hornet*, with specially lightened aircraft and almost twice the normal fuel load, after hitting their targets in Japan the aircraft then flew on to crash-land in China or Russia.

Two major variants were the B-25C and B-25D, both powered by the 1268kW (1700hp) R-2600-13, and fitted with wing racks for external fuel tanks. They could carry a maximum bombload of 2359kg (5200lbs), including 113kg (250lb) bombs externally. A torpedo could also be carried. Both served in the RAF as the Mitchell Mk II (the Mk I had failed to make any impact in the RAF), and several hundred went to the Soviet Union.

The B-25G had a crew of four, two of whom were required to load and fire the 75mm (2.9in) gun mounted in its nose for use against shipping. The B-25H with five crew was an improved version, with a lighter 75mm (2.9in) gun and no less than eight 12.7mm (0.5in) machine-guns mounted on its nose, as well as the other defensive armament. It could also carry rockets and a bombload of 1361kg (3000lbs).

The final production variant was the R-2600-29-powered B-25J, which had the 75mm (2.9in) gun removed, and an additional crew member. In later versions, the bombardier's position was removed, and eight 12.7mm (0.5in) machine-guns installed in a solid nose. Some 275 were supplied to the RAF as Mitchell Mk IIIs, and examples of all the variants served with the US Navy and Marine Corps.

Lockheed P-38J Lightning

Specification

Country of origin: USA

Powerplant: Two 1063kW (1425hp) Allison V-1710-89/91 in-line piston engines

Armament: One 20mm (0.79in) Hispano M2(C) cannon with 150 rounds, and four 12.7mm (0.5in) Colt-Browning MG 53-2 machine-guns with 500 rounds per gun, plus two 726kg (1600lb) bombs or ten 12.7mm (0.5in) rockets

Weight: 5800kg (12,780lbs) empty; 9798kg (21,600lbs) loaded

Dimensions: 15.85m (52ft) span; 11.53m (37ft 10in) length; 2.99m (9ft 10in) height; 30.42m² (327.5sq ft) wing area

Performance: 666km/h (414mph) at 7620m (25,000ft); 13,410m (44,000ft) ceiling; 5 minutes to 4572m (15,000ft) climb

Flight range: 3701km (2300 miles) with drop tanks

Crew: One

The first of the three famous US fighter aircraft of World War II (the others being the P-47 and P-51), the Lockheed P-38 owed its unusual design to the 1937 requirement that it could fly at 580km/h (360mph) for one hour at 6095m (20,000ft). No single-engine design was capable of this performance at that time, so H.L. Hibbard and his team came up with the twin-boom configuration. The resulting XP-38 prototype first flew in January 1939, and it performed well enough to win a contract for 13 YP-38 aircraft before crashing during a crossing of the USA. Powered by 858kW (1150hp) Allison V-1710-27/29 engines, the YP-38s were armed with one 37mm (1.4in) cannon, two 12.7mm (0.5in) and two 7.62mm (0.3in) machine-guns. However, the first production variant, the P-38, which entered service in mid-1941, reverted to the armament of the XP-38 – namely, one 23mm (0.9in) cannon and four 12.7mm (0.5in) machine-guns – although it also had greater protection for the pilot. They were largely used for training duties.

The first combat-ready variant was the P-38D with self-sealing tanks, which began to enter service in August 1941. The P-38E used a 20mm (0.79in) Hispano cannon, and served largely in the south-west Pacific and the Aleutian Islands near Alaska, although a pilot based in Iceland claimed the first USAAF victory after shooting down an Fw 200 Condor. The RAF expressed interest in the new fighter, and ordered no less than 667 Lightning Mk Is in March 1940. However, after testing, the RAF pilots recommended cancellation of the order, and so the vast majority was absorbed by the USAAF, the USA having now joined the war.

The P-38F had uprated engines and provision for two underwing racks for bombs or drop tanks. The P-38G was essentially the same, bar its 988kW (1325hp) V-1710-51/55 engines, and came into service in 1943. Shortly afterwards, the P-38H with 1063kW (1425hp) engines made its debut in Europe, where the type had earned the German nickname, 'the fork-tailed devil'. With the introduction of the P-38J in August 1943, the type increasingly worked on ground-attack tasks in Europe, but retained its fighter status in the Far East and Pacific.

In 1944, the arrival of the P-38L, which became the most numerous of all the variants, saw the Lightning able to carry unguided rockets for the first time, and it could now deliver two 907kg (2000lb) bombs. The P-38 was even used as a tactical bomber, with the lead aircraft in a formation carrying a bombardier in the nose. The last significant variant was the P-38M, the night-fighter version, which came too late to see action in Europe, but caught the last few weeks of the conflict in the Pacific. It had two seats, with the radar operator in a raised rear cockpit, and the radar mounted under the nose.

Douglas A-20 Havoc/Boston

Specification for A-20G

Country of origin:	USA
Powerplant:	Two 1193kW (1600hp) Wright R-2600-23 Double Cyclone radial piston engines
Armament:	Six forward-firing, 12.7mm (0.5in) Browning machine-guns, three 12.7mm (0.5in) machine-guns in turrets, and up to 1364kg (3000lb) bombload
Weight:	7265kg (15,984lbs) empty; 12,338kg (27,200lbs) loaded
Dimensions:	18.69m (61ft 4in) span; 14.63m (48ft) length; 5.36m (17ft 7in) height; 43.11m² (464sq ft) wing area
Performance:	546km/h (339mph) at 3780m (12,400ft); 7865m (25,800ft) ceiling
Flight range:	1754km (1090 miles)
Crew:	Three

The A-20 was designed to saturate fixed enemy defences in the front line with bombs, but in the event, the fast-moving German blitzkrieg forces meant that no target stayed in place long enough. At the same time, the bombers had to be heavily protected by fighters, or else risk heavy losses. The outbreak of war in 1939 prompted both the RAF and French Air Force to bulk order many American aircraft, one of which was the A-20, known as the Boston in RAF service. As a consequence, production was beginning to reach full flow when the USA joined the war in December 1941. The prototype DB-7 flew on 17 August 1939, and deliveries began to the French Air Force the following year. Most of these aircraft, however, would end up with the RAF after the Fall of France.

Judged unsuitable for the bombing role, about 100 RAF Boston Mk II aircraft were converted to the night-fighter role in the winter of 1940–41, by fitting an AI Mk IV radar, additional armour, flame-damping exhaust pipes, and eight machine-guns. Known as the Havoc, it was also involved in a number of experiments to counter the German bombing effort, such as trailing aerial mines on a long wire in front of enemy bomber streams. Lacking a purpose-built night-fighter, the USAAF also converted A-20s for service in the Pacific in 1942, designating the variant the P-70. This achieved limited success before being replaced by the P-61 in 1944.

From 1941 onwards, the conventional A-20 was used as a 'light-medium' bomber, attacking forward road and railway bridges, vehicle parks and advanced air bases, and later as a close-support aircraft, softening up enemy defences before attacks by ground forces. The RAF's Bostons were heavily used during the cross-Channel raids between 1942 and 1944, and found a niche providing smokescreens for amphibious landings. They had one or two machine-guns in a dorsal position for self-defence.

The first variant to enter USAAF service was the A-20A, followed by the A-20B, of which 999 were built. The A-20C had the ability to carry torpedoes. The A-20G deleted the bomb aimer's position, which had become largely superfluous, and installed a battery of cannons or machine-guns in a solid nose. Up to eight 12.7mm (0.5in) machine-guns could be carried in such a situation. Up to a total of 1814kg (4000lbs) of bombs could also be carried, either internally or on wing racks. The A-20H was similar to the 20G model, but had uprated 1268kW (1700hp) R-2600-29 engines. The last operational variants in service were the A-20J and A-20K, which were fitted with a new, frameless, glazed nose.

A-20s were widely used in the Pacific as low-level attack aircraft, using fragmentation bombs over Japanese shipping and airfields. An F-3A reconnaissance variant, of which some 46 were converted from A-20J and A-20K aircraft, had widespread use in the same theatre. RAF Boston Mk IVs and Vs saw service as close-support aircraft up to the end of the war in Italy.

Martin B-26G Marauder

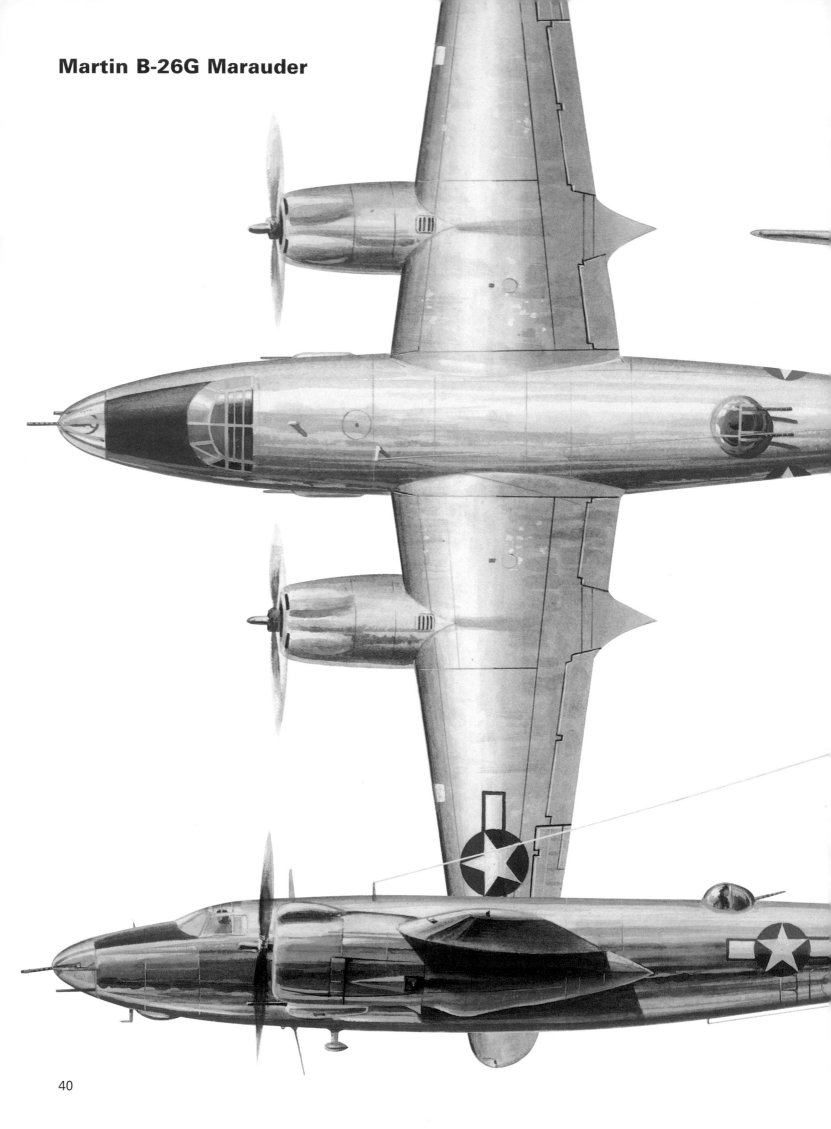

Specification

Country of origin: USA

Powerplant: Two 1432kW (1920hp) Pratt & Whitney R-2800-43 Twin Wasp radial piston engines

Armament: Eleven 12.7mm (0.5in) machine-guns, and up to 1818kg (4000lb) bombload

Weight: 11,475kg (25,300lbs) empty; 17,327kg (38,200lbs) loaded

Dimensions: 21.64m (71ft) span; 17.09m (56ft 1in) length; 6.2m (20ft 4in) height; 61.13m² (658sq ft) wing area

Performance: 454km/h (283mph) at 1524m (5000ft); 6035m (19,800ft) ceiling

Flight range: 1770km (1100 miles)

Crew: Seven

In January 1939, the USAAC asked manufacturers to submit proposals for a new medium bomber to replace the Martin B-10 and Douglas B-18, capable of delivering a 907kg (2000lb) bombload at high speed over a long range. Martin's response was the twin-engined Martin 179, which was immediately ordered into production in September 1939. Armed with two 12.7mm (0.5in) and two 7.62mm (0.3in) machine-guns, this five-man bomber was powered by two 1380kW (1850hp) Pratt & Whitney R-2800-5 Double Wasp engines, and designated the B-26. Although its bombload was 2631kg (5800lbs) and it had a top speed of 507km/h (315mph), the B-26's design meant that it had a high take-off and landing speed, which, coupled with the unusual tricycle landing gear, caused difficulties for pilots new to the aircraft. The first 200 or so examples were therefore used for training, and the first deliveries of the new type did not reach the USAAF until 1941.

Later that year, production switched to the B-26A, which could carry a 550mm (22in) torpedo or extra fuel tanks in its bomb-bay, and all its defensive guns became 12.7mm (0.5in). It was this variant that operated against New Guinea from Australia, saw service in the Middle East with the RAF as the Marauder Mk I, and later fought in the Battle of Midway as a torpedo-bomber. By that time (mid-1942), the most numerous variant, the B-26B, began to enter service. The B-26B-1 had improved armour and engine cowlings, and new ventral and tail-gun positions. The B-2, -3 and -4 all had the uprated R-2800-41/43 engine. The B-4 had a longer nosewheel to try to reduce take-off speeds, and beam guns instead of the ventral position, while the B-5 had slotted flaps to slow down the landing speed.

In an attempt to help improve the situation further, the B-10 had a longer wing span and was fitted with a package of four fixed, 12.7mm (0.5in) machine-guns on the nose, and a powered tail turret. At the same time, the tail was increased in size to improve lateral stability. Aircraft built at Martin's new factory in Omaha, Nebraska, which were of B-10 standard were designated B-25Cs, and some of them served with the South African Air Force in the desert as Marauder Mk IIs.

Neither the B-26D or E were produced, the next variant to see service being the B-26F, with a wing with an increased angle of 3.5 degrees, which improved its take-off and landing behaviour, but reduced maximum speed to 446km/h (277mph). It first entered service in February 1944, and again some went to the South African Air Force, designated Marauder Mk IIIs. The same designation was applied to the B-26Gs which were bought by the UK, although the B-26G was little different to the earlier F, the only changes being minor ones to equipment and fittings.

Consolidated B-24J Liberator

Specification

Country of origin: USA

Powerplant: Four 895kW (1200hp) Pratt & Whitney R-1830-43 Twin Wasp radial piston engines

Armament: 10 12.7mm (0.5in) Browning machine-guns, and a normal bombload of 3992kg (8800lbs)

Weight: 16,556kg (36,500lbs) empty; 29,484kg (65,000lbs) loaded

Dimensions: 33.52m (110ft) span; 20.47m (67ft 2in) length; 5.49m (18ft) height; 97.36m² (1048sq ft) wing area

Performance: 467km/h (290mph) at 7620m (25,000ft)

Flight range: 3220km (2000 miles) with 3992kg (8800lb) bombload

Crew: Ten

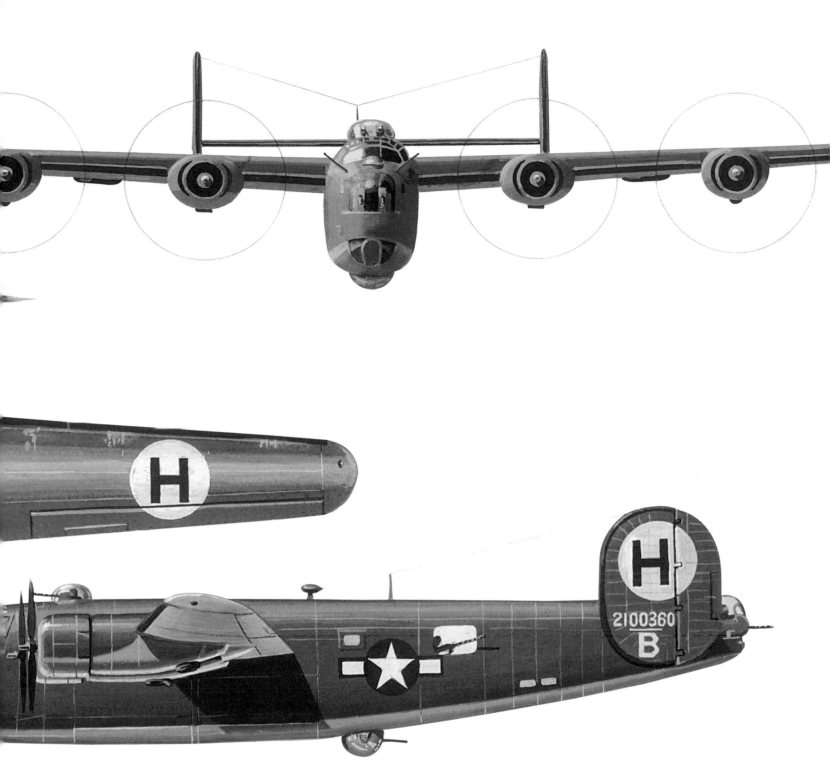

Although the first prototype did not fly until 1939, the Liberator was to play a major role in the Allied war effort against Germany. In 1938, Consolidated's chief engineer, Isaac M. Laddon, decided to design a new bomber, the Model 32, around David R. Davis's new wing, which, it was claimed, would produce 10 to 25 per cent less drag than other wings. The US Army Air Corps contracted Laddon to build his new design, called the XB-24, requesting that it be capable of 483km/h (300mph), 10,670m (35,000ft) and a range of 4828km (3000 miles). In March 1939, the French Air Force ordered 175 Model 32s, designated the 32B7, but France fell before they could be delivered, and the RAF picked up this batch in 1941 as the Liberator Mk I, along with 139 of their own order, designated the Liberator Mk II and fitted out to British requirements. Due to its long range, the aircraft was used in a variety of roles, including transport and training, but also with Coastal Command, equipped with the ASV Mk I radar and as bombers in the Middle East and India.

The first mass-produced variant for the USAAF was the B24D (only a few of the B-24A- and C-series were ever built). Powered by the Dash-43 engines, the aircraft had a bombload of 3992kg (8800lbs) and 10 12.7mm (0.5in) machine-guns to defend itself with. The B-24D saw

service in every theatre of the war, and was the most important long-range bomber in the Pacific in 1942–43. It also performed a vital task in closing the gap in the middle of the Atlantic in which the U-boats had been able to operate unchecked. The B-24D was known as the Mk III in RAF service (Mk IIIa if it was a Lend-Lease aircraft). The Mk V used by Coastal Command had retractable chin and ventral radars, and extra specialist equipment. A 20-seat transport variant, the C-87 Liberator Express, was designed and built virtually overnight in order to evacuate the Dutch East Indies in the face of the Japanese advance. The B-24E (RAF Mk IV) had Curtiss propellers, but was little different. The B-24G had a nose turret fitted as standard, while the B-24H (RAF Mk VI) was the designation for contracts placed in 1941 and early 1942. The B-24J was a rationalization of the modifications made to the G- and H-series, with a new autopilot and bombsight. The B-24L had an improved turbocharger and lightweight, twin-gun tail 'stinger' instead of a turret. The last major wartime variant was the B-24M.

A single-tailed variant, the B-24N, was ordered, but the end of the war saw the contract cancelled. Independently, the US Navy designed its own single-tailed version, the PB4Y-2 Privateer, used primarily for maritime patrol in the last year of the war.

Vought F4U-1A Corsair

First flown in May 1940, the Corsair remained in production for 12 years, a mark of the quality of this bent-winged fighter. In 1938, the US Navy issued a requirement for a high-performance, shipboard fighter, and the Corsair was the submission of the Vought-Sikorsky company. Powered by the 18-cylinder Pratt & Whitney Double Wasp engine, which drove a 4.04m (13ft 4in) propeller, the Corsair was a huge aircraft for a fighter, and its famous, inverted gull-wing shape was adopted purely to give the propeller more ground clearance. An extremely strong aircraft, its large wings allowed it to fly at the slow speeds required for carrier landings, yet in October 1940 a top speed of 652km/h (405mph) was recorded, faster than any other fighter in the world at that time.

The first production Corsair, the F4U-1, was delivered to the US Navy on 31 July 1942, armed with six 12.7mm (0.5in) machine-guns. However, various handling traits meant that it was not accepted for carrier service by the US Navy, and the first batches went to the US Marine Corps, who quickly demonstrated the type's superiority over the Japanese fighter aircraft of the time. Production of the aircraft grew slowly to begin with, but almost 2300 were built in 1943, by which time all had come to appreciate the aircraft's talents. From the 1550th example onwards, the Corsair was equipped with the more powerful 1679kW (2250hp) Pratt & Whitney R-2800-8W engine, which used water injection; this variant was designated the F4U-1A. Other modifications included a bulge in the cockpit canopy above the pilot's head to improve forward vision – never good with such a huge engine in front – which, in turn, was later replaced with a clear, raised canopy and a raised seat for the pilot.

The F4U-1B was a variant ordered by the British Fleet Air Arm, who had begun to use the Corsair from early 1943. Although the US Navy still had not cleared the Corsair for carrier operations, the British introduced it into service on the tiny convoy escort carriers, so small that the Corsairs in Fleet Air Arm service had to have 20cm (8in) cut off each wing to fit below the deck. The F4U-1C, of which 200 were built, were armed with four 20mm (0.79in) M2 Hispano cannon, giving it a greater punch. The F4U-1D, on the other hand, was capable of carrying either two 454kg (1000lb) bombs or two 606litre (160 USgal) drop tanks. A night-fighting version of the Corsair, the F4-U2, was equipped with radar and autopilot, and although only 32 were converted, they achieved some notable successes. Apart from the disappointing F4U-3 high-altitude fighter, the last wartime model was the F4U-4, powered by the R-2800-18W/-42W engine, and capable of mounting air-to-ground rockets. The F4U-4B was identical in all respects, apart from its four M3 cannon.

Specification

Country of origin:	USA
Powerplant:	One 1679kW (2250hp) Pratt & Whitney R-2800-8W radial piston engine
Armament:	Six 12.7mm (0.5in) Browning MG 53-2 machine-guns with 400 rounds per gun, plus two 454kg (1000lb) bombs or eight 127mm (5in) rockets
Weight:	3944kg (8695lbs) empty; 5032kg (11093lbs) loaded
Dimensions:	12.5m (41ft) span; 10.16m (33ft 5in) length; 4.9m (16.1ft) height; 29.17m² (314sq ft) wing area
Performance:	671km/h (417mph) at 6065m (19,900ft); 11,427m (36,900ft) ceiling
Flight range:	1633km (1015 miles)
Crew:	One

North American
P-51D Mustang

Perhaps surprisingly, the greatest American fighter of the war was first ordered by the British Purchasing Commission in 1940. North American had never produced a fighter before, and the BPC gave them only 120 days in which to do it. In fact, the prototype NA-73 was built from scratch in 102 days, although they had to wait three weeks for the 857.6kW (1150hp) Allison V-1710-39 in-line engine. It first flew on 26 October 1940, although the British had ordered 320 examples of the XP-51 on 29 May 1940. The Mustang Mk I flew its first combat mission on 27 July 1942. However, the engine's performance was not good, and the Mustang was then largely used for ground-attack and reconnaissance, supporting the disastrous Dieppe raid soon after entering service. Nevertheless, the USAAF ordered 150 cannon-armed, 20mm (0.79in) P-51s, and 310 P-51As, with the 895kW (1200hp) V-1710-81 engine and four 12.7mm (0.5in) machine guns, as well as two underwing racks for 227kg (500lb) bombs. The P-51A was designated the Mustang Mk II in RAF service.

By this time, the RAF had taken the logical step of matching the excellent airframe of the P-51 with the Rolls-Royce Merlin engine, which immediately produced a top speed of over 644km/h (400mph). North American decided to build a Mustang powered by the Packard

licence-built Merlin. In the meantime, the USAAF ordered the A-36A, an attack version used mainly in Italy and Sicily, and identical to the P-51A except for some faulty dive-brakes. The P-51B, (known in RAF service as the Mustang Mk III, was the first production Mustang to be fitted with the Merlin, followed by the P-51C, armed with six 12.7mm (0.5in) machine-guns.

Visibility from the cockpit had been improved on the Mustang Mks II and III, which used the bulged Malcolm hood used on the RAF's Spitfires. However, the P-51D, introduced in 1943, used the classic bubble canopy that had first been adopted on the F6 reconnaissance variant, and had a dorsal fin to improve stability. The P-51D gave the Allies a fighter that could take on the best the Luftwaffe could offer on equal or better terms, and was a significant factor in winning and maintaining air superiority. In the RAF, the D-series aircraft was known as the Mk IV. Later versions had a fuel tank added behind the pilot, which gave the aircraft the ability to escort the bombers to Berlin and beyond. Although several other experiments were tried, none except the lightweight P-51H, with a four-bladed propeller and taller tail, saw combat – the latter's small taste of action consisting only of a few missions flown out of the Philippines before VJ Day.

Specification

Country of origin:	USA
Powerplant:	One 1264kW (1695hp) Packard V-1650 Merlin in-line piston engine
Armament:	Six 12.7mm (0.5in) Browning MG 53-2 machine-guns with 400 rounds per gun for the inboard pair of guns, and 270 rounds per gun for the outboard pairs, plus two 227kg (500lb) or 454kg (1000lbs) bombs or six 127mm (5in) rockets
Weight:	3232kg (7125lbs) empty; 5488kg (12,100lbs) loaded
Dimensions:	11.29m (37ft 1in) span; 9.83m (32ft 3in) length; 2.64m (8ft 8in) height; 21.65m² (233sq ft) wing area
Performance:	703km/h (437mph) at 7620m (25,000ft); 12,770m (41,900ft) ceiling
Flight range:	3347km (2080 miles) with drop tanks
Crew:	One

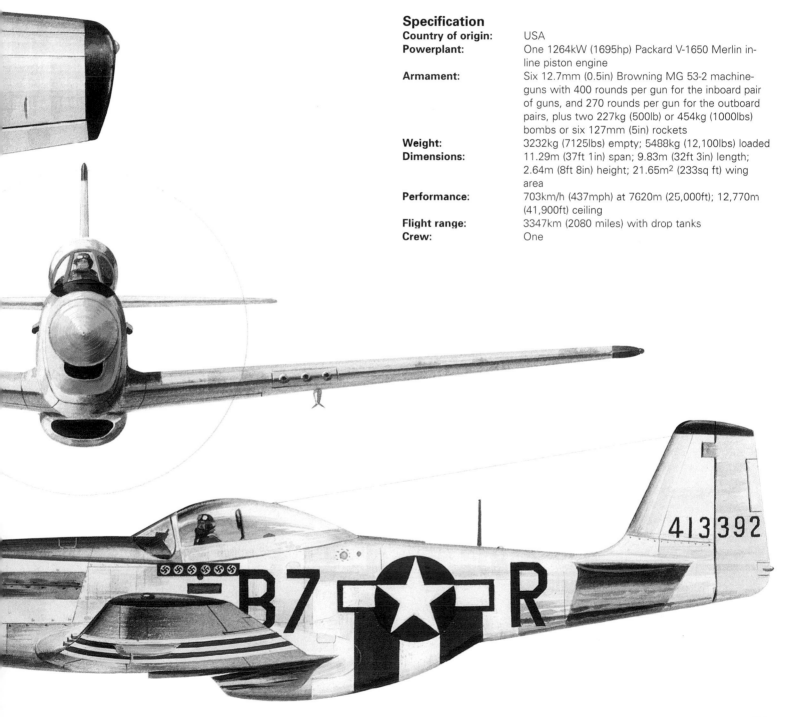

Republic P-47M Thunderbolt

Nicknamed the Juggernaut or 'Jug' for short, the P-47 Thunderbolt was a giant compared to other contemporary fighters, and, in its later versions, the P-47 was considerably heavier than a laden Dornier Do 17 bomber. The P-47 was designed and built by Alex Kartveli around its engine, the massive 18-cylinder R-2800, which came equipped with a turbocharger, and which drove a 3.71m (12ft 2in) diameter, four-blade propeller. The aircraft was armed with no less than eight machine-guns, with at least 350 rounds each, an unprecedented amount of firepower for an Allied fighter at that stage of the war.

The first prototype flew on 6 May 1941, only eight months after it had first been ordered. Despite teething problems, the aircraft's potential was clear, and the US Army ordered 171 examples, quickly followed by an order for another 602 of an improved model, the P-47C. The P-47B was delivered in 1942, but only flew its first escort mission from the UK in April 1943. The P-47 pilots found life hard when dogfighting with the German Bf 109s and Fw 190s, but they could easily out-dive their opponents and escape trouble. The P-47C had its engine mounted almost 30cm (1.2ft) further forward, which helped correct a balance problem, and provision was made for mounting either a 757litre (200 USgal) drop tank or 227kg (500lb) bomb. Pilots quickly came to appreciate the aircraft's ability to soak up punishment and still make it back to base.

The most numerous variant, the P-47D, of which over 12,600 were built, began to reach front-line units in mid-1943. (The P-47G was the essentially identical version built by Curtiss-Wright.) The P-47D incorporated a wide range of improvements, including a refined engine with water injection, multi-ply tyres, improved pilot protection, and a better turbocharger installation. A 'universal' wing was introduced to later P-47Ds, which allowed them to carry 454kg (1000lb) bombs on two wing points, as well as the centreline load. Carrying three drop tanks gave the P-47 the legs to escort the US bombers all the way to their target for the first time, and it became commonplace for returning fighters to shoot up any targets of opportunity when returning to base. By the final year of the war, this activity had resulted in the P-47 becoming the chief Allied ground-attack aircraft, with examples serving in the Pacific and over Burma with the RAF, as well as in Europe. From July 1943, a bubble canopy similar to that fitted to the RAF's Typhoon ground-attack aircraft was fitted to the P-47, which significantly improved the pilot's visibility, and from batch D-35-RA onwards, 10 12.7cm (5in) rockets could be carried under the aircraft's wings.

Only two other service variants were produced: the P-47M, a P-47D with a modified engine capable of 811km/h (504mph), intended to catch the V1 flying bomb and other German jets and rockets; and the extremely long-range P-47N, using integral-wing fuel tanks for the first time to provide a long-range fighter for the Pacific theatre.

Specification

Country of origin: USA

Powerplant: One 2088kW (2800hp) Pratt & Whitney R-2800-57 radial piston engines

Armament: Eight 12.7mm (0.5in) Browning machine-guns, with 425 rounds per gun

Weight: 4728kg (10,423lbs) empty; 7031kg (15,500lbs) loaded

Dimensions: 12.42m (40ft 9in) span; 11.02m (36ft 4in) length; 4.47m (14ft 7in) height; 27.87m² (300sq ft) wing area

Performance: 811km/h (504mph); 13,411m (44,000ft) ceiling

Flight range: 901km (560 miles) without drop tank

Crew: One

227386

Grumman TBF Avenger

Built as a replacement for the Douglas TBD Devastator, the Grumman TBF Avenger was to be the main torpedo bomber of the Pacific war. The design was drawn up by Bob Hall, the chief experimental engineer at Grumman, in response to a demanding US Navy requirement for a long-range, single-engined torpedo-bomber. Unusually, it had an internal weapons bay with a defensive position at the end, and a powered turret with a single 7.62mm (0.3in) machine gun. The bombardier could face forward to deliver bombs from medium altitudes and above, or turn around and man the lower defensive position, which also had a machine-gun. The pilot, seated high up in the aircraft with an excellent view, had his own forward-firing, 7.62mm (0.3in) machine-gun. The TBF could carry either four 227kg (500lb) bombs or one Mk 13 torpedo in its bomb-bay, or, if necessary, extra fuel tanks. The wings were designed to tuck back alongside the fuselage when on board a carrier, and, naturally, it was equipped with an arrester hook at its tail.

The prototype, the XTBF-1, first flew on 1 August 1941, powered by the 1268kW (1700hp) Wright R-2600-8 radial engine, although almost 300 examples had already been ordered by the US Navy. The second prototype was being rolled out when news of Pearl Harbor reached the plant, and the type was appropriately named the Avenger. Its combat debut came at the Battle of Midway, on 4 June 1942, when six

aircraft set out from USS *Hornet*, but only one made it safely back.

The British Fleet Air Arm bought a first batch of 395 Avengers, all modified with British equipment and fittings, and designated TBF-1B Tarpons (the name was later dropped). In total, over 900 Avengers served with the British in both the Atlantic and Pacific Oceans. The good handling of the Avenger, despite its ponderous looks, prompted the development of the TBF-1C, which replaced the single nose gun of the TBF-1A with two 12.7mm (0.5in) guns mounted in the wings. The TBF-1J had bad-weather avionics and lighting fitted, along with special anti-ice protection.

In response to massive demand for the new aircraft, in 1942 production began at General Motors, whose aircraft were designated the TBM. The TBM-3 was the most numerous variant (equivalent to the TBF-3), powered by the Wright R-2600-20 engine, with provision for wing-mounted rockets or drop tanks, and an externally mounted arrester hook. The heavy, powered turret was often deleted in these models to improve performance. The TBF/M-1D, TBM-3D and -3E had a pod-mounted RT-5/APS-4 search radar under their right wing. Other radar fits were common, including the Westinghouse ASB, and the automatic, low-level APG-4 'Sniffer' bombing radar. The latter used a special dipole array towed out under each wing at an angle of 40 degrees. When radar was fitted, the bombardier was also tasked with the role of radar operator.

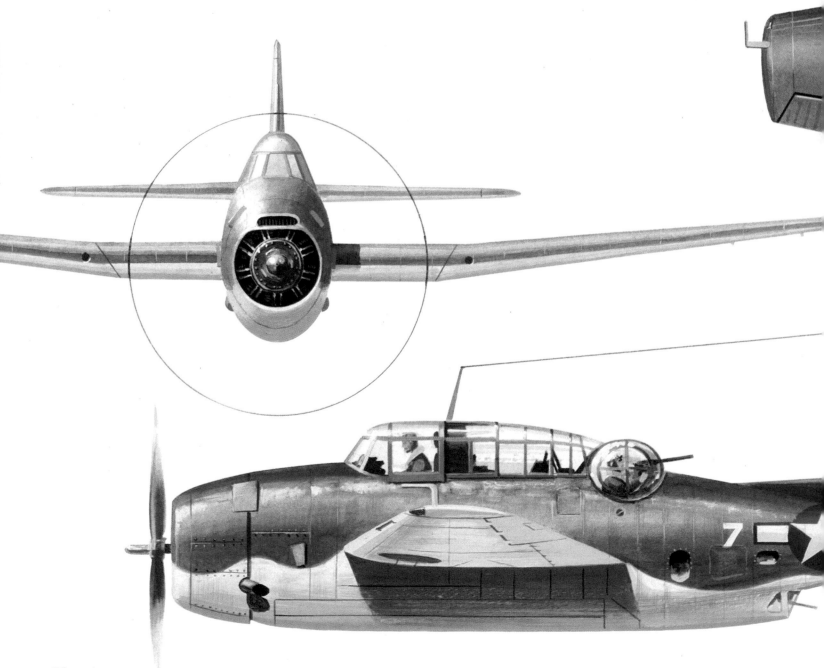

Specification for TBF-1

Country of origin: USA

Powerplant: One 1268kW (1700hp) Wright R-2600-8 radial piston engine

Armament: One 12.7mm (0.5in) Browning machine-gun, and two 7.62mm (0.3in) machine guns, plus an internal bay for one 577mm (22.7in) torpedo, or 907kg (2000lbs) of other stores

Weight: 4788kg (10,555lbs) empty; 7876kg (17,364lbs) loaded

Dimensions: 16.51m (54ft 2in) span; 12.2m (40ft) length; 5m (16ft 5in) height; 45.52m^2 (490sq ft) wing area

Performance: 436km/h (271mph); 6830m (22,400ft) ceiling

Flight range: 1778km (1105 miles)

Crew: Three

Grumman F6F Hellcat

The most important American fighter aircraft of the war in the Pacific, the Hellcat did not even enter combat service until 31 August 1943. Although the F4F Wildcat had proved that it could hold its own against the Japanese fighters, it was lacking in speed and overall performance, and it was decided to build an improved Wildcat. Initially, two prototypes were built, the XF6F-1 and the XF6F-2, with different Wright R-2600 engines, but it was decided to use the Pratt & Whitney R-2800 Double Wasp, which equipped the F4U Corsair. The wings, the largest used on any single-engined fighter of World War II, were able to pivot backwards and fold alongside the fuselage, a technique used in other Grumman aircraft. The armament comprised six 12.7mm (0.5in) machine-guns.

The XF6F-1 first flew in June 1942, exhibiting a few minor teething problems. These were resolved by the time of the first production aircraft, the F6F-3, powered by the 1492kW (2000hp) R-2800-10 engine. The XF6F-4 flew in October of the same year with the R-2800-27 engine, but this powerplant was not adopted. As air combat in the Pacific tended to take place at low or medium altitudes, turbochargers were not adopted, but the level of armour was slightly increased on the production models. Provision was made for the aircraft to carry a drop tank beneath the centreline, and some were later modified to carry rockets or bombs on external racks.

The US Navy fighter squadron VF-9 was the first to receive the F6F on USS *Essex* in January 1943, although the type did not see combat until August of that year, during the attack on Marcus Island. At the end of 1943, radar was installed on F6Fs for night-fighting work. The radars used were the APS-4 and APS-6, which were mounted in a pod far out on the starboard wing. Although the F6F's speed was reduced by some 32km/h (20mph), the pod did not adversely affect the aircraft's handling. The first night-fighter was the F6F-3E, which was converted in the field, but it was soon followed by the production F6F-3N with radio altimeter and red cockpit lighting.

The F6F-3N was fitted with the R-2800-10W engine, which had water injection, and this engine also powered the F6F-5, produced from 21 April 1944, with minor modifications to the F-3 design. So many were produced that, at their height, the production lines were delivering 20 aircraft a day, almost faster than the pilots could be trained; it dominated the Pacific air battle from August 1943 onwards. A F6F-5N night-fighter version was produced, along with an F6F-5P photo-reconnaissance variant, all of which (including the standard fighter F-5) had the two inner machine-guns replaced with 20mm (0.79in) cannon. All F-5s could carry external ordnance, whether extra fuel, or bombs or rockets.

The British Fleet Air Arm bought a substantial number of F-3s and F-5s, calling them the Hellcat Mk I (initially Gannet before 1944) and Mk II respectively.

Specification for F6F5

Country of origin: USA

Powerplant: One 1492kW (2000hp) Pratt & Whitney R-2800-10W Double Wasp radial piston engine

Armament: Six 12.7mm (0.5in) Browning machine-guns, plus 907kg (2000lb) bombload or six 127mm (5in) rockets

Weight: 4191kg (9239lbs) empty; 5670kg (12,500lbs) loaded

Dimensions: 13.08m (42ft 10in) span; 10.23m (33ft 7in) length; 3.9m (13ft 1in) height; 31.03m² (334sq ft) wing area

Performance: 621km/h (386mph) at medium altitudes; 11,369m (37,300ft) ceiling

Flight range: 1674km (1040 miles)

Crew: One

Boeing B-29 Superfortress

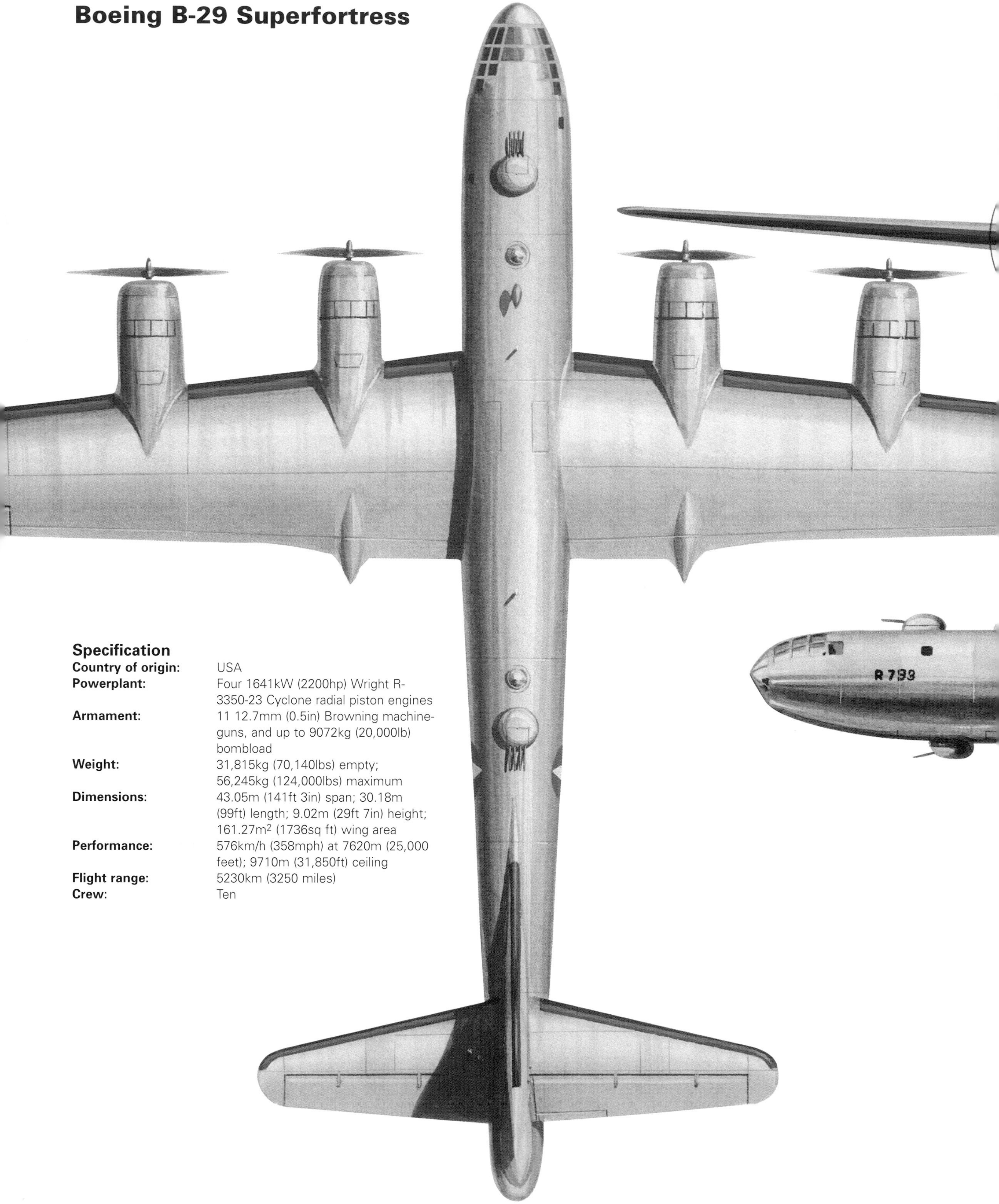

Specification

Country of origin: USA

Powerplant: Four 1641kW (2200hp) Wright R-3350-23 Cyclone radial piston engines

Armament: 11 12.7mm (0.5in) Browning machine-guns, and up to 9072kg (20,000lb) bombload

Weight: 31,815kg (70,140lbs) empty; 56,245kg (124,000lbs) maximum

Dimensions: 43.05m (141ft 3in) span; 30.18m (99ft) length; 9.02m (29ft 7in) height; 161.27m² (1736sq ft) wing area

Performance: 576km/h (358mph) at 7620m (25,000 feet); 9710m (31,850ft) ceiling

Flight range: 5230km (3250 miles)

Crew: Ten

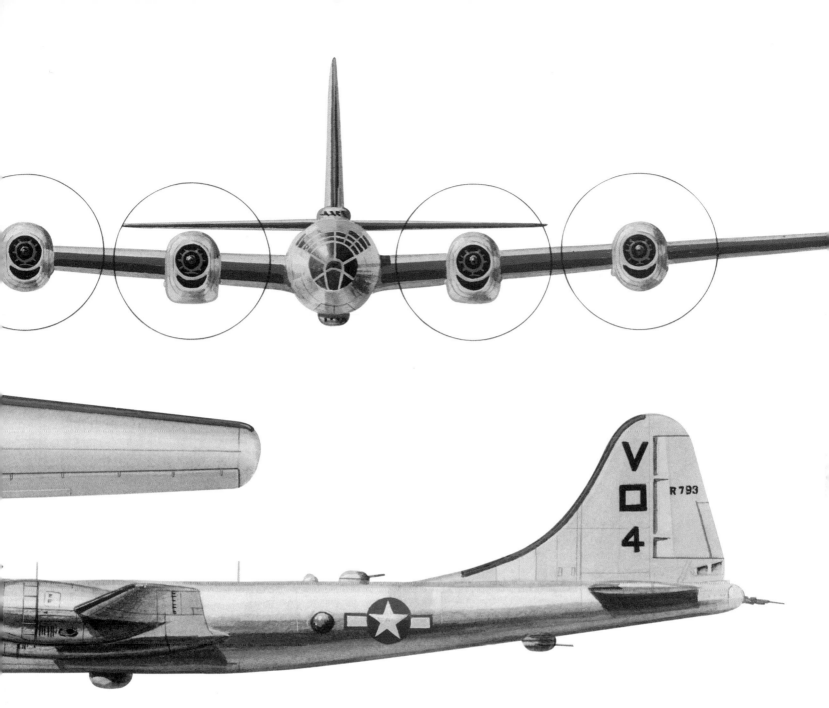

When 'Enola Gay' performed her mission on 6 August 1945, the world realized that warfare would never be the same, but the B-29, like its payload that day, had overcome a long and difficult development process. First mooted in 1938, as a replacement for the B-17 bomber which had recently entered service, the requirement was for a pressurized, high-altitude bomber capable of 628km/h (390mph) and a range of 8582km (5333 miles). However, it was not popular in the War Department, and struggled for funding before the outbreak of war.

Although Boeing was used to building large aircraft (the pre-war XB-15 experimental prototype had passageways in its wings large enough to stand up in), the design of the new bomber took some time to come together. The two pressurized cabins, fore and aft, were linked by a tunnel above the two huge bomb-bays, while the wing was made as narrow as possible to reduce drag. More armour was added to the design, along with self-sealing tanks and powered gun turrets. Huge flaps were added to allow the aircraft to take off and land at slower speeds, but they were still double the length required for the B-17, meaning that long runways were a necessity. Four Wright-3350 Duplex Cyclones, with two turbochargers each, were used to drive 5.05m (16ft 7in) diameter propellers. The defensive armament was two upper, and two lower, twin, 12.7mm (0.5in) machine-gun turrets, controlled from sighting stations around the aircraft, and a gunner in a tail position armed with two 12.7mm (0.5in) guns and a 20mm (0.8in) cannon with 100 rounds.

After the Japanese surprise attack on Pearl Harbor, a huge manufacturing programme was initiated for the B-29, despite the fact that the prototype was yet to fly. In fact, the XB-29 did not take off on its first flight until 21 September 1942, but once it had flown it was clear that the B-29 would be the only weapon in the US aerial arsenal capable of reaching Japan. The aircraft had numerous teething problems that required fixing – the first 175 examples had their (almost) 10,000 faults fixed in the aptly named 'Battle of Kansas', where the maintenance took place. Once in the air, however, the coldness of the atmosphere at 10,060m (33,000ft) helped prevent breakdowns.

The B-29 was not an easy aircraft to fly, thanks to its complexity. Crews had to be trained to take advantage of the aircraft's complex systems and difficult handling characteristics. However, the first raid on Japan took off on 15 July 1944, and soon B-29s were taking off from specially prepared airstrips all over the Pacific. The B-29A was equipped with a four-gun front turret to improve defensive armament, and a wider wingspan of some 30cm (12in), but the lack of serious fighter opposition at this stage of the war encouraged the deployment of the B-29B, which, echoing a number of field conversions, stripped all defensive weaponry – save that in the tail – in a bid to save weight. A number of B-29s were converted to F-13A standard for long-range reconnaissance.

Fairey Swordfish Mark I

Specification

Country of origin:	Great Britain
Powerplant:	One 515kW (690hp) Bristol Pegasus III M.3 radial piston engine
Armament:	One 45.7cm (18in), 730kg (1610lb) torpedo or 680kg (1500lb) mine or six 113kg (250lb) bombs, plus two 7.7mm (0.303in) machine-guns
Weight:	2132kg (4700lbs) empty; 3406kg (7510lbs) loaded
Dimensions:	13.87m (45ft 6in) span; 10.87m (35ft 8in) length; 3.76m (12ft 4in) height; 56.69m² (607sq ft) wing area
Performance:	222km/h (138mph) at 2438m (8000ft); 5867m (19,250ft) ceiling
Flight range:	879km (546 miles)
Crew:	Three

The 'Stringbag', as it was popularly known, was already approaching obsolescence by the time war broke out, and by rights should have been replaced in service before it had the chance to do half what it did during the conflict. A biplane in a monoplane's war, it looked like a relic, but was held in great affection by its crews, and performed consistently for the Fleet Air Arm. First flown as a prototype in April 1934, it showed enough promise to be awarded a contract for 86 aircraft to be known as the Swordfish. The Swordfish Mk I was powered by a 515kW (690hp) Bristol Pegasus IIIM radial engine. It was armed with one forward-firing, 7.7mm (0.303in) machine-gun, and another in the aft cockpit. It could carry one 450mm (18in) torpedo of 730kg (1610lbs), or one 680kg (1500lb) mine, or two 227kg (500lb) bombs beneath the centreline, with another two 113kg (250lb) bombs on wing racks. The type entered service in 1936, and by 1938, all the Fleet Air Arm's torpedo-bomber squadrons were equipped with it.

The Swordfish did not see action until 1940, when, with extra fuel tanks in the rear cockpit, it was increasingly used on raids on German-held Channel ports. Its crowning moment, however, was the raid on Taranto in November 1940, which severely damaged three Italian battleships, and hit a cruiser and two destroyers, thus giving the Royal Navy the upper hand in the Mediterranean. The attempt in 1942 to repeat such success against the *Scharnhorst, Gneisenau* and *Prinz Eugen* ended in tragedy – not one of the six Swordfish returned, although the flight commander, Lt Commander Esmonde, was awarded the Victoria Cross, the first member of Fleet Air Arm to be so recognized.

As a result of this failure, the Swordfish gave up its role as a torpedo-bomber, and turned to anti-submarine duties, using depth-charges, or in the case of the Swordfish Mk II, with its strengthened lower wing, rockets. Later examples of the Mk II were equipped with the more powerful Pegasus XXX engine. The final production version, the Swordfish Mk III, had a radome between its (fixed) undercarriage legs, which carried a scanner for its ASV Mk X radar, but in other respects it was the same as the Mk II. The final variant was the Mk IV, which was a Mk II with an enclosed cockpit for operations over the cold Canadian waters.

The Swordfish continued to give good service up to the end of the war, one 'Stringbag' managing to sink no less than four U-boats whilst protecting a convoy; no less than 2391 examples of all types were built.

Gloster Gladiator

The least well known of the fighters on the RAF's active list during the Battle of Britain, the biplane Gladiator was clearly a product of the inter-war years. Although in the mid-1930s, monoplanes were the coming thing, the Gloster designer, H. P. Folland, looked at how the design of the Gloster Gauntlet fighter could be improved, and built a prototype, the SS.37, powered by the Bristol Mercury engine, as a private venture. It was capable of 380km/h (236mph), which was later improved when the 481kW (645hp) Mercury VIS was fitted in late 1934 to 389km/h (242mph). In 1935, it was flown to Martlesham Heath for official evaluation, which resulted in an order for 35 Gladiators. It was to be powered by the 626kW (840hp) Mercury IX, and fitted with an enclosed cockpit and four machine-guns. The first examples of the Gladiator Mk I were delivered to the RAF in February and March 1937, all equipped with Lewis guns attached under the wings, although later Mk Is could accept either the Lewis, Vickers or the licence-built Colt-Browning.

The Gladiator Mk II was fitted with a 619kW (830hp) Mercury VIIIA engine with electric starter. Thirty-eight examples were fitted with arrester hooks and transferred to serve with the Fleet Air Arm in December 1938, replacing the Hawker Nimrods and Ospreys pending the arrival of

purpose-built Sea Gladiators. As well as the hook, these had catapult attachment points, and a ventral stowage fairing for a dinghy. The early defence of Malta was performed by Sea Gladiators, later named Faith, Hope and Charity by a journalist, although there were actually four of them, and they were flown by the RAF. Perhaps remarkably, there were considerable foreign sales to Belgium, China, Eire, Greece, Latvia, Lithuania , Norway and Sweden, most of which were Mk Is.

Although most front-line fighter units had re-equipped with the Spitfire or Hurricane by September 1939, two squadrons of Gladiators were sent to France with the British Expeditionary Force, and others were involved in the Norwegian campaign. A flight protected Falmouth during the Battle of Britain, as it was the only RAF fighter capable of operating from the nearest aerodrome, although no German bombers were shot down by the Gladiator during that infamous summer. Others served in the Middle East, claiming some success against Italian biplanes in North Africa between March and October 1940. After they were finally retired from the front line, they were used for communications and liaison duties by the RAF, and Coastal Command used a number for meteorological purposes until 1944. The Gladiator was the last biplane fighter in RAF service.

Specification for Gladiator Mk II

Country of origin:	Great Britain
Powerplant:	One 619kW (830hp) Bristol Mercury IX radial piston engine
Armament:	Four 7.7mm (0.303in) machine-guns
Weight:	1562kg (3444lbs) empty; 2206kg (4864lbs) loaded
Dimensions:	9.83m (32ft 3in) span; 8.36m (27ft 5in) length; 3.53m (11ft 7in) height; 30.01m² (323sq ft) wing area
Performance:	414km/h (257mph) at 4450m (14,600ft); 10,211m (33,500ft) ceiling
Flight range:	708km (440 miles)
Crew:	One

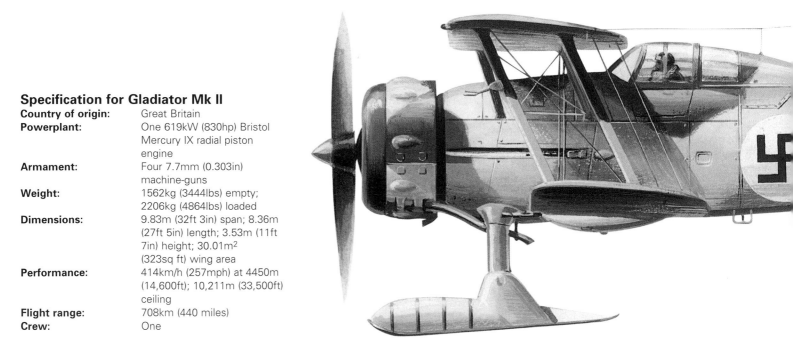

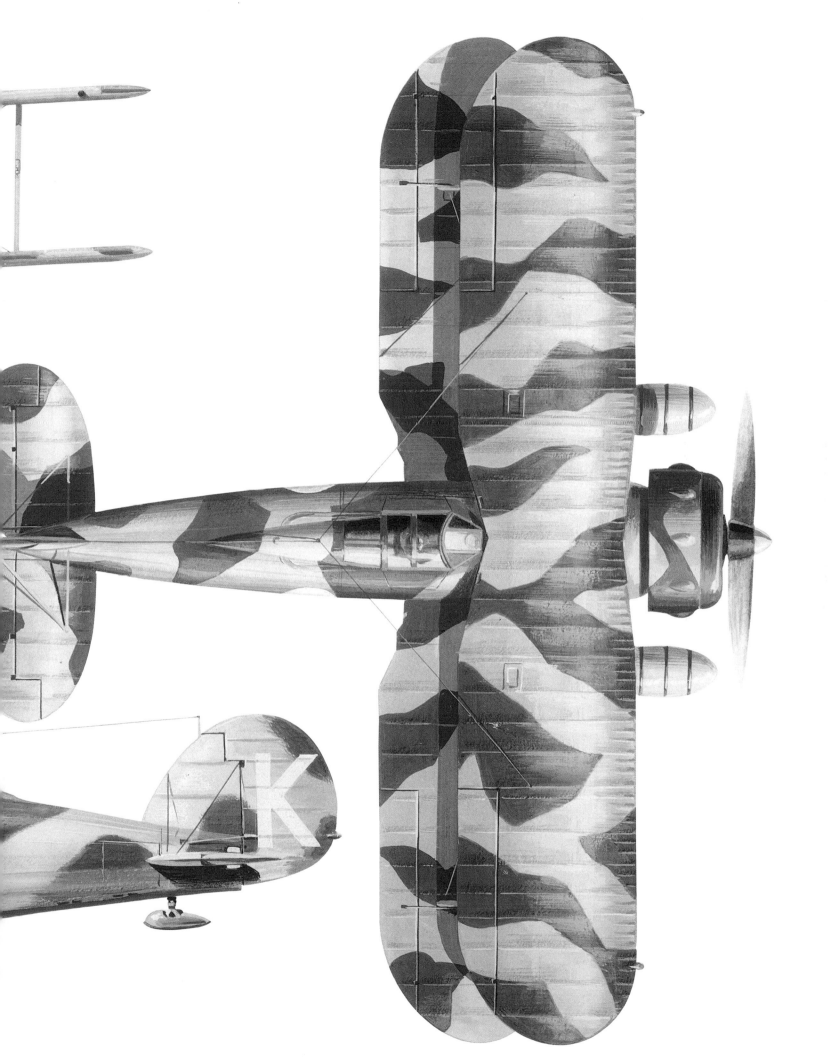

Bristol Blenheim IV

Specification

Country of origin: Great Britain

Powerplant: Two 686kW (920hp) Bristol Mercury XV 9-cylinder radial piston engines

Armament: One 7.7mm (0.303in) Vickers, one 7.7mm (0.303in) Browning machine-gun, and up to 454kg (1000lb) bombload

Weight: 4445kg (9790lbs) empty; 6537kg (14,400lbs) loaded

Dimensions: 17.17m (56ft 4in) span; 12.98m (42ft 7in) length; 2.99m (9ft 10in) height; 43.57m² (469sq ft) wing area

Performance: 428km/h (266mph) at 3595m (11,800ft); 8310m (27,260ft) ceiling

Flight range: 2340km (1454 miles)

Crew: Three

Lord Rothermere, proprietor of the *Daily Mail*, requested in 1934 that the Bristol Aeroplane Company build him a light, fast transport for commercial use. The Bristol Type 142, designed by Frank Barnwel, was powered by two Bristol Mercury engines, and first flew on 12 April 1935. It was found to be 48km/h (30mph) faster than Britain's latest fighter aircraft, which caused a furore. The Air Ministry asked if they could test it, and Lord Rothermere presented it to the nation. An order for 150 examples of a militarized version was placed that same year. The changes were to add a bomb-aimer's station, a bomb-bay and a dorsal turret. The first aircraft reached the RAF in March 1937, and in July, a follow-on order for what had now become known as the Blenheim Mk I was issued. The powerplant was two 626kW (840hp) Bristol Mercury VIII engines, giving enough power to carry three crew and a maximum of 454kg (1000lbs) of bombs. Armament was a 7.7mm (0.303in) machine- gun in the port wing, and a single Vickers machine-gun in the dorsal turret.

Although they were largely replaced in the bombing role before the outbreak of war, the Mk I continued to serve as a conversion trainer and, later, as the Mk IF, night-fighter, equipped with the AI Mk III or IV radar set, and four 7.7mm (0.303in) machine-guns mounted in a pack under the fuselage. Blenheim Mk Is were sold to Finland, Turkey, Yugoslavia and Romania, meaning that they were also used against the Allies.

Towards the end of 1938, the Blenheim Mk IV was put into production, having an extended nose section and increased fuel tankage in the wings, supplying two Bristol Mercury XV engines. Defensive armament was increased, the dorsal turret now mounting two guns and a rear-facing, twin-gun chin mounting, which was remotely controlled. Armour was increased, and two external wing racks added. The Blenheim Mk IV served in large numbers in most theatres of the war, performing sterling service in the early desert campaigns, for example. They were sturdy aircraft, and capable of absorbing some punishment.

The last variant, briefly known as the Bisley, was introduced in mid-1942 as the Blenheim Mk V. It was originally intended to be a low-altitude, close-support aircraft, but was used as a high-altitude bomber. It featured a revised nose section and some updated equipment, but was little different from the Mk IV. It served in the Middle and Far East, but did little of great note. It was promptly withdrawn after being moved to the Italian front, where its losses were too high to be acceptable.

Hawker Hurricane Mk II

Although perceived as the less glamourous of the two major RAF fighters during the Battle of Britain, the Hawker Hurricane in fact outnumbered the Spitfire during 1940, and shot down more Luftwaffe aircraft. Its dated fabric and wood construction also allowed it to absorb more punishment than the Spitfire, pilots often returning safely home with pieces of fabric flapping loose. The Hurricane was an attempt by the designer Sydney Camm to produce a monoplane version of the successful Hawker Fury biplane, powered by the ubiquitous Rolls-Royce Merlin engine. The prototype first flew in November 1935, reaching a top speed of 507km/h (315mph) at 4575m (15,000ft), and the Hurricane was subsequently ordered into production the following year, armed with eight Browning machine-guns. As the RAF raced to re-equip before war broke out, little change was made to the design, but new propellers were fitted, and the 768kW (1030hp) Merlin III became the engine used by 1939. Export sales had also been good, with licence production in Yugoslavia and Belgium, and several other nations buying examples.

The Hurricane accompanied the British troops to France in 1939, whilst the Spitfire stayed at home; it did, however, see action in Norway and during the battle for France the following year. During the Battle of Britain, it tended to leave the Messerschmitt Bf 109s to the Spitfires, which could match it in performance, but the Hurricane was an excellent gun-platform and possessed the tightest turn circle of all the aircraft in the skies over England.

In September 1940, the Hurricane II began to appear, powered by the two-stage, supercharged Merlin XX, which delivered 883kW (1185hp), enough for a top speed of 550km/h (342mph). The Mk IIA Series 2 had the ability to carry underwing fuel tanks, or a pair of 113kg (250lb) bombs, an ability that was used on sweeps over Europe in early 1941.

The Mk IIB flew with a 12-gun wing, all 7.6mm (0.3in) Brownings, and became known as the Hurribomber. The Mk IIC was equipped with four 20mm (0.79in) cannon instead, but both saw extensive service in the Middle and Far East, as well as Europe. The majority of the Hurricane Mk IID variants built, however, saw service in the North African desert and later Burma, armed with 40mm (1.6in) anti-tank guns under each wing.

All the Hurricanes that were supplied to hotter climes were fitted with a Vokes air filter, which reduced their performance by some eight per cent, but cut down on maintenance. Hurricane Mk IIs performed sterling service as night fighters in 1941 and 1942. The Mk II was also delivered in some numbers to the Soviet Union.

The last RAF Hurricane variant was the Mk IIE, which was soon redesignated the Hurricane Mk IV. Fitted with the 954kW (1280hp) Merlin 24 or 27, it had a universal wing capable of mounting rockets, anti-tank guns or any other external store. A number of early Hurricanes were adapted to be launched from catapults on the prow of merchant ships, but later the Mk IIC was converted to the Sea Hurricane Mk IIC, with an arrester hook and other special naval equipment, and these served with distinction for the Fleet Air Arm.

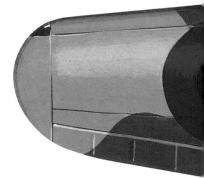

Specification

Country of origin:	Great Britain
Powerplant:	One 955kW (1280hp) Rolls-Royce Merlin XX in-line piston engine
Armament:	Two 20mm (0.79in) Hispano cannon with 120 rounds per gun, four 7.7mm (0.303in) Browning machine-guns with 350 rounds per gun, and one 227kg (500lb) or two 113kg (250lb) bombs
Weight:	2313kg (5100lbs) empty; 3078kg (6785lbs) loaded
Dimensions:	12.19m (32ft 3in) span; 9.82m (32ft 2in) length; 3.99m (13ft 1in) height; 23.92m² (257.5sq ft) wing area
Performance:	541km/h (336mph) at 3810m (12,500ft); 10.850m (35,600ft) ceiling
Flight range:	740km (460 miles)
Crew:	One

Supermarine Spitfire LF VB

Specification

Country of origin: Great Britain

Powerplant: One 1182kW (1585hp) Rolls-Royce Merlin 45M in-line piston engine

Armament: Two 20mm (0.79in) Hispano cannon with 120 rounds per gun, four 7.7mm (0.303in) Browning machine-guns with 350 rounds per gun, and one 227kg (500lb) or two 113kg (250lb) bombs

Weight: 2313kg (5100lbs) empty; 3078kg (6785lbs) loaded

Dimensions: 9.94m (32ft 7in) span; 9.1m (29ft 11in) length; 3.47m (11ft 5in) height; 22.48m² (242sq ft) wing area

Performance: 575km (357mph) at 1829m (6000ft); 11,125m (36,500ft) ceiling; 1 minute 36 seconds to 1524m (5000ft) climb

Flight range: 1593km (990 miles) with drop tanks

Crew: One

Undoubtedly the most famous British aircraft of World War II, the Supermarine Spitfire was the brainchild of R. J. Mitchell. Initially called the Type 300, it was a private venture that drew heavily on Mitchell's experience in building winning designs for the Schneider seaplane trophy. It was powered by another private venture, the Rolls-Royce PV.12, which evolved into the Merlin. Worried by the latest German fighters, and impressed by the Type 300, the Air Ministry ordered it into production in June 1936. No.19 Squadron was the first to receive the Spitfire Mk I in August 1938, and by mid-1940, 19 squadrons were operating the type, although many were lost over Dunkirk. A twin, cannon-armed, 20mm (0.79in) variant, the Mk IB, served in limited numbers during the Battle of Britain, as did the Mk II, powered by the Merlin 12 engine. The Mk V entered service in early 1941, equipped with the Merlin 45, which gave it a much-improved performance, and these Spitfires were used on sweeps over occupied France. Most were Mk VBs, with two 20mm (0.79in) cannon and four machine-guns mounted in a 'clipped' wing that improved roll rate, but later the Mk VC emerged, which could have just four 20mm (0.79in) cannon. The Mk V was the first variant to be allowed to serve overseas, fighting in the desert and in the defence of Malta and Australia. It was also adapted to carry either one 227kg (500lb) bomb or two 113kg (250lb) bombs.

By 1942, Rolls-Royce had developed the Merlin 61, which gave the Spitfire a maximum speed of 666km/h (414mph), with much-improved climb rate and altitude performance. The Mk IX was introduced in July 1942, and was essentially a Mk VC with the new engine bolted on, and an extra fuel tank. The Mk VIII, with the same engine, but redesigned fuselage, were all sent overseas. The next major variant was the Packard-built Merlin 266-powered Mk XVI, which served only in Europe, and was usually armed with two 20mm (0.79in) cannon and two 12.7mm (0.5in) machine-guns.

The Mk XII was powered not by the Merlin, but by the 1294kW (1735hp) Rolls-Royce Griffon IIB engine, with the four 20mm (0.79in) cannon armament and clipped wings. It was used to intercept low-level raiders, and to conduct fighter sweeps over Europe. The Mk XIV was an interim model used to intercept V1 flying bombs, before the entry into service of the major Griffon Spitfire variant, the Mk 21, which had a Griffon 61 installed driving a five-blade propeller. In later versions of this and other Spitfires still in production, a teardrop canopy was introduced with a cut-down rear fuselage to improve visibility.

As each Spitfire variant entered service, an equivalent reconnaissance version was also produced, and the PR (photo-reconnaissance) Spitfires were a significant intelligence asset for the Allies throughout the war.

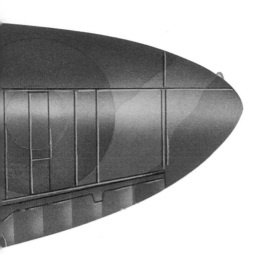

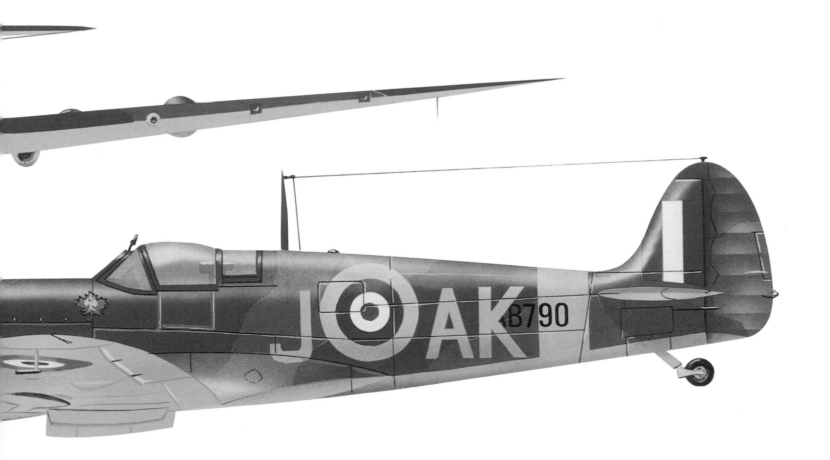

Hawker Typhoon IB

Despite a highly unpromising start in its intended role as an interceptor, the Hawker Typhoon went on to become one of the mainstays of the RAF, performing the role of ground-attack aircraft with distinction. Sydney Camm, designer of the Hurricane, realized in 1937 that the RAF would soon be looking for a replacement for the fighter, and this was confirmed by the Air Ministry later that year, when it issued a requirement for a 12-gun fighter. The 24-cylinder Napier Sabre engine was nominated by the Ministry to be the powerplant of this new fighter. The Typhoon prototype flew in February 1940, but this was quickly overshadowed by events in Europe, prompting the RAF to focus on its current Spitfire and Hurricane fighters. A further problem emerged on 9 May 1940, when a structural failure caused part of the fuselage to break away, which delayed progress by a month. The first production Typhoon Mk IA was flown on 27 May 1941, armed with the required 12 machine-guns.

Only a short while before, however, the second prototype had flown with a very different armament: four 20mm cannon, and production aircraft of this type were therefore designated the Typhoon Mk IB, which gradually outnumbered the Mk IA. The type entered RAF service with No 56 Squadron in September 1941, but the accident rate was extremely high and, after much testing, Hawker discovered that airframe fatigue caused the whole tailplane to break away, a flaw that had killed many pilots. It took almost a year for all the type's problems to be ironed out. By this time, the RAF was not happy with the aircraft's rate of climb or performance at high altitude; however, the Typhoon had shown itself to be very good at low level, particularly tackling hit-and-run Focke-Wulf Fw 190s. A new engine, the 1626kW (2180hp) Sabre IIA, and the provision to carry two bombs on underwing racks transformed the Typhoon into an excellent fighter-bomber, used by day and night in the intruder role.

By late 1943, the classic combination of Typhoon and unguided rockets had been brought together, and in such a configuration, the aircraft proved deadly to German positions and targets of opportunity before and after D-Day. Typhoons patrolled in 'Cab Ranks', waiting to be called into action by ground troops against any difficult opposition and, as a consequence, they were much feared by the Germans. In the last year of the war, the Sabre IIB, and then the Sabre IIC engines were introduced. There were only a few variants of this wartime classic: a single NF.Mk IB night-fighter, which was converted in late 1941 from a fighter-bomber and carried an AI Mk VI interception radar; and a small number of tactical reconnaissance aircraft designated Typhoon FR.Mk IB, although one version had two vertical cameras, and the other had a forward-facing camera instead of one of its cannon.

Specification

Country of origin: Great Britain

Powerplant: One 1626kW (2180hp) Napier Sabre II liquid-cooled H-24 in-line piston engine

Armament: Four 20mm (0.79in) Hispano Mk 1 cannon with 140 rounds per gun, plus two 454kg (1000lb) bombs or eight 27.2kg (60lb) rockets

Weight: 3993kg (8800lbs) empty; 6341kg (13,980lbs) loaded

Dimensions: 12.67m (41ft 7in) span; 9.73m (31ft 10in) length; 4.66m (15ft 4in) height; 25.92m² (279sq ft) wing area

Performance: 652km/h (405mph) at 5485m (18,000ft); 10,365m (34,000ft) ceiling; 6 minutes 12 seconds to 4570m (15,000ft) climb

Flight range: 820km (510 miles) with bombs

Crew: One

De Havilland DH.98 Mosquito

Specification B.Mk XVI

Country of origin:	Great Britain
Powerplant:	Two 1253kW (1680hp) Rolls-Royce Merlin 72 V-12 in-line piston engines
Armament:	Four 227kg (500lb) bombs internally, and two more under the wing, or one 1814kg (4000lb) bomb
Weight:	6638kg (14,635lbs) empty; 10,433kg (23,000lbs) loaded
Dimensions:	16.51m (54ft 2in) span; 12.47m (40ft 11in) length; 3.81m (12ft 6in) height; 42.18m² (454sq ft) wing area
Performance:	656km/h (408mph) at 7925m (26,000ft); 11,280m (37,000ft) ceiling
Flight range:	2389km (1485 miles)
Crew:	Two

The Mosquito was one of the stars of World War II, yet it was almost cancelled three times. The designers' intention was always to make an aircraft out of wood, powered by two Merlin engines, with a small bomb-bay, that would be fast enough to outrun enemy fighters, and thus not need defensive armament of its own. However, the Air Ministry was suspicious of its all-wood construction, and it was with great reluctance it agreed to the production of a prototype for a reconnaissance version. When it was officially tested in February 1941 at Boscombe Down, the Mosquito reached 631km/h (392mph), over 32km/h (20mph) faster than any RAF fighter; it went into service as the photo-reconnaissance Mosquito PR.Mk I.

In 1942, the F.MkII night-fighter went into production, equipped with an AI Mk IV radar and four 20mm (0.79in) Hispano cannon, and four 7.7mm (0.303in) machine-guns in the nose. At the same time, the B.Mk IV bomber went into production, able to carry four 227kg (500lb) bombs in its bomb bay. The Series II was used as a specialist bomber or for pathfinding activities, using the Oboe navigational aid to guide Bomber Command's aircraft to their targets. The PR.Mk IV was a reconnaissance version of this aircraft.

By 1943, bomber production had switched to the B.Mk IX, powered by two-stage Merlins, and capable of better high-altitude performance. A bulged bomb-bay allowed both the B.Mk IX and B.Mk IV Special to carry a 1814kg (4000lb) bomb, whilst the B.Mk XVI was designed to carry it from the outset, and with a pressurized cockpit to allow high-altitude operations.

The most numerically important version was the FB. Mk VI fighter-bomber, which had a short bomb bay for two 113kg (250lb) bombs, with wing racks for two more. The Series II had the ability to carry double the bombload, or unguided rockets, and it was this version, alongside the 57mm (2.2in) gun-armed FB Mk XVIII, that was the main attack weapon of Coastal Command from mid-1943 onwards.

The Mosquito was also very active as a night-fighter, introduced into service as the NF.Mk XII, XIII, XVII, XIX and NF.Mk XXX, with increasingly advanced electronics, including radar and electronic-warfare devices. The NF.Mk XXX operated in the last year of the war, often accompanying the RAF's 100 Group, which specialized in deceiving German anti-aircraft defences.

Photo-reconnaissance was another important role for the Mosquito, variants including the PR.Mk IV, VIII, IX, XVI and XXXIV. The Mk IX was the first to be used heavily by Allied intelligence. By mid-1943, it was flying daily over occupied Europe, to the extent that it flew 3000 sorties in four months at the end of the year. By the time that the Mk XVI was introduced in the last year of the war, its high-altitude performance was such that it could operate unmolested above German airspace. Like the Spitfire, the Mosquito was used by a large number of Allied nations, and continued to serve after the war.

Avro Lancaster B.1

Specification

Country of origin: Great Britain

Powerplant: Four 1223kW (1460hp) Rolls-Royce Merlin XXII in-line piston engines

Armament: Eight 7.7mm (0.303in) Browning machine-guns, and one 9979kg (22,000lb) bomb, or up to 6350kg (14,000lb) bombload

Weight: 16,738kg (36,900lbs) empty; 31,751kg (70,000lbs) loaded

Dimensions: 31.09m (102ft) span; 21.18m (69ft 6in) length; 6.1m (20ft 6in) height; 120.49m² (1297sq ft) wing area

Performance: 462km/h (287mph) at 3505m (11,500ft); 7470m (24,500ft) ceiling

Flight range: 4070km (2530 miles) with 3175kg (7000lb) bombload

Crew: Seven

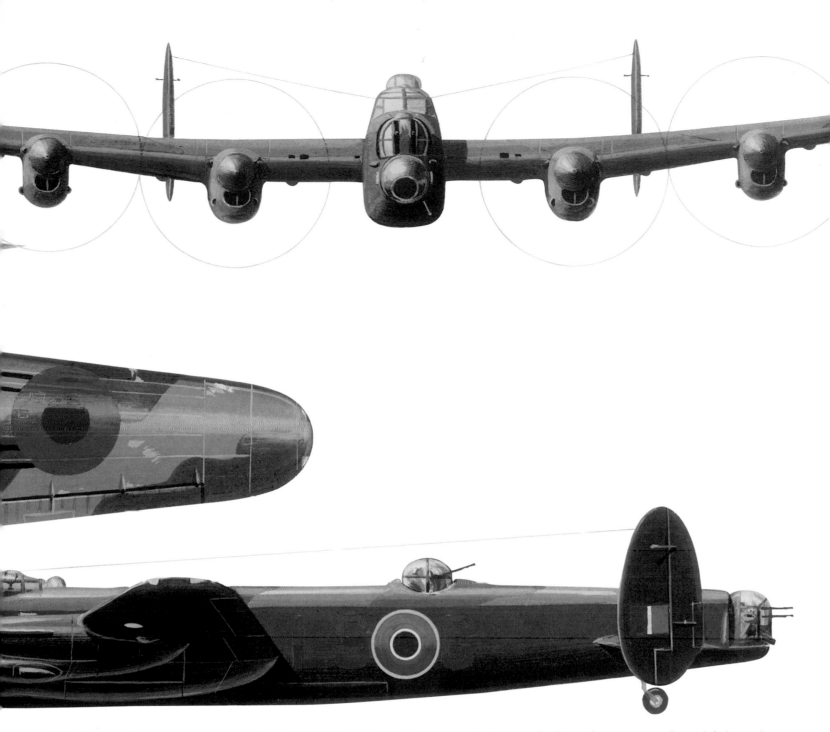

In 1940, the Avro Manchester entered service with the RAF, powered by two Rolls-Royce Vulture engines. Unfortunately for the Manchester, the Vulture was plagued with problems, but the basic design had proved itself sound. It was decided to develop a four-engined version, designated the Manchester Mk III, which would be fitted with four Rolls-Royce Merlin engines. Although the Air Ministry wanted Avro to build the Merlin-powered Halifax instead, Avro argued that it would be quicker for them to build their Manchester conversions, which were redesignated the Lancaster, and were soon to outnumber their rival.

In fact, the Air Ministry was so impressed with the Lancaster that they cut their order for the Manchester, and the first Lancaster Mk I flew on 31 October 1941. The first operational sortie, a minelaying sortie over the Heligoland Bight, was carried out by No. 44 Squadron. The aircraft was kept secret until 17 August 1942, when seven of the 12 aircraft that raided the U-boat engine plant at Augsburg failed to return, despite the mission's success. As a result, the RAF switched permanently to night attacks. Over time, the Lancaster was adapted to carry the 3632kg (8000lb) bomb, and later the 5448kg (12,000lb) bomb, the maximum bombload rising to 6350kg (14,000lbs). Later production Mk 1s were fitted with the 1201kW (1610hp) Merlin 24s to cope with this increase in weight.

The Lancaster Mk II was a stopgap intended to deal with the shortage of Merlin engines in 1941. It carried the more powerful Bristol

Hercules radial engines, but its performance was always inferior to the Mk Is, and the last Mk II mission was carried out on in September 1944. The engine supply problem was addressed by allowing it to be built overseas. The Lancaster Mk III was powered by US-built Packard-Merlin engines, but was otherwise identical to the Mk I in all respects. Defensive armament changed a little, but not significantly. Various mid-upper turrets were tried, while by the end of the war, the four 7.7mm (0.303in) Brownings were replaced by a turret with a small radar set for automated aiming, and two 12.7mm (0.5in) machine-guns. A version with minor equipment changes was built in Canada as the Mk X, and served with Canadian crews based in the UK.

From mid-1942 onwards, the Lancaster was to be Bomber Command's main weapon. It was adaptable enough to be used for specialist missions, such as the Dambuster raids in May 1943, and the 5448kg (12,000lb) Tallboy raids of 1944 against targets such as the *Tirpitz*. The heaviest bomb dropped by the Lancaster was the gigantic 9988kg (22,000lb) Grand Slam. By the later stages of the war, many Lancasters were converted to carry the H2S bombing radar.

The Mk VI was used as a pathfinder, powered by Merlin 83s, which gave better performance at altitude. The last two variants were the B. Mk I (FE) and B. Mk VII(FE), which were tropicalized variants intended for use against Japan, but the war ended before they saw service. The Lancaster Mk IV, which first flew in June 1944, went on to serve as the Avro Lincoln after the war.

Gloster Meteor

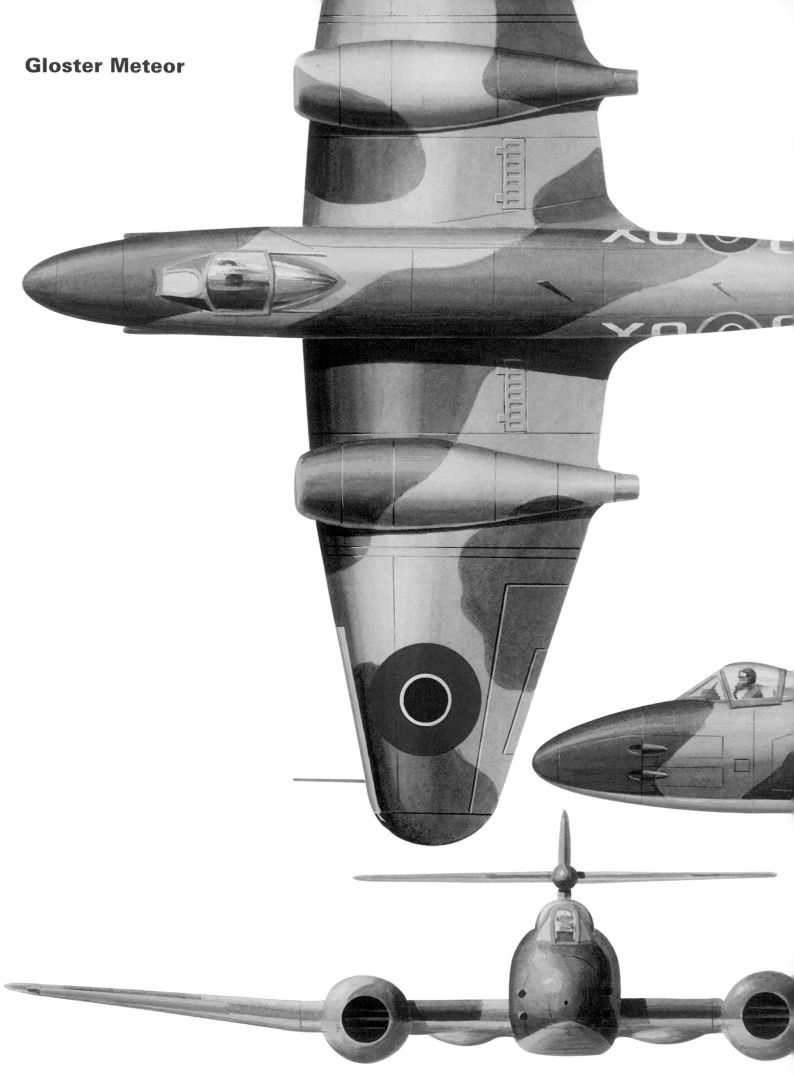

The only Allied jet fighter to reach operational status in World War II, the Meteor went on to have a long, distinguished service with the RAF. The first British jet to fly was the Gloster E.28/39, powered by the Frank Whittle-designed W.1 gas turbine, and this type's success led the British Air Ministry to issue a requirement for a jet-powered fighter aircraft. In response to this, George Carter designed the Gloster Meteor, which, like its German counterpart, the Me 262, was powered by two engines, due to the low thrust available at this early stage of jet engine development. No less than eight prototypes were built, using seven different power sources. The first used Rover W.2B engines, the second Power Jets W.2/500s, the third Metrovick F.2 axial-flow turbojets, the fourth W.2B/23 engines, the fifth Halford/de Havilland H.1s, the sixth, the prototype Meteor Mk II, DH Goblin engines, the seventh the same engines, but with modified rudder and fins, and the eighth Rolls-Royce W.2B/37 Derwent Is.

The first prototype was completed and underwent taxying trials in July 1942 near the Newmarket race course, but it was the fifth prototype that was the first to fly from Cranwell, on 5 March 1943. The first production batch of 20 Meteors, designated the Meteor Mk I, were completed with Rolls-Royce W.2B/23 Welland 1 reverse-flow turbojets with centrifugal-flow compressors. The Wellands were capable of producing 771kg (1700lbs) of thrust, and the top speed of the Meteor was 668km/h (415mph). Armament was four 20mm (0.79in) Hispano cannon in the nose, although there was provision for up to six to be fitted. Deliveries began to No.616 Squadron in July 1944, and the Meteor was initially used to intercept the V1 flying bombs then being launched with frequency against England. The first successful interception of a V1 by a Meteor took place on 4 August 1944. The type was also used to train USAAF bomber crews in techniques to counter the Me 262, which was beginning to enter Luftwaffe service in considerable numbers.

Once the flying-bomb threat had diminished, the squadron moved to Belgium, where it was joined by No.504, Squadron flying the improved Meteor Mk III, equipped with a sliding hood. However, the Meteors were initially banned from crossing the front lines, and as, by this late stage of the war, Luftwaffe aircraft rarely ventured into Allied airspace (most being shot down before having the opportunity to do so), the chances of meeting a German fighter were virtually nil. There is no recorded instance of a Meteor meeting a Me 262 in combat.

Specification

Country of origin:	Great Britain
Powerplant:	Two 771kg (1700lb) Rolls-Royce Welland 1 turbojets
Armament:	Four 20mm (0.79in) Hispano cannon in the nose
Weight:	3692kg (8140lbs) empty; 6257kg (13,795lbs) loaded
Dimensions:	13.11m (43ft) span; 12.57m (41ft 3in) length; 3.96m (13ft) height; 34.74m² (374sq ft) wing area
Performance:	668km/h (415mph) at 3050m (10,000ft); 12,190m (40,000ft) ceiling
Flight range:	1610km (1000 miles)
Crew:	One

Mitsubishi G3M 'Nell'

Specification for G3M2 Model 22

Country of origin:	Japan
Powerplant:	Two 801.6kW (1075hp) Mitsubishi Kinsei 45 14 cylinder radial piston engines
Armament:	Three 7.7mm (0.303in) Type 92 machine-guns, and one 20mm Type 99 cannon, plus 800kg (1764lb) bombload
Weight:	4965kg (10,946lbs) empty; 8010kg (17,659lbs) loaded
Dimensions:	25m (82ft) span; 16.45m (54ft) length; 3.685m (12ft 1in) height; 75m^2 (807.32sq ft) wing area
Performance:	374km/h (232mph) at 4200m (13,780ft); 9130m (29,954ft) ceiling
Flight range:	4380km (2722 miles)
Crew:	Seven

The Mitsubishi G3M was a ubiquitous aircraft that had already experienced extensive use in combat before Pearl Harbor, and saw wide service in the early years of the war. As early as July 1935, in response to an Imperial Japanese Navy requirement for a land-based, twin-engined, reconnaissance aircraft, Mitsubishi flew the Ka-15 prototype, which revealed its potential to be converted into a long-range medium bomber. Some 21 prototypes and pre-production aircraft were built, fitted with the Type 1 and later Kinsei 2 radial engine. Following excellent flight trials, production began in June 1936. Designated the Navy Type 96 Attack Bomber Model 11, the G3M1 was powered by two 678.6kW (910hp) Kinsei 3 radial engines, giving it a maximum speed of 360km/h (224mph) at 1975m (6480ft). After 34 had been built, the arrival of the Kinsei 41 and 42 engines in 1937 prompted the development of the G3M2 (Model 21) variant, which became the most numerous, with 581 built by mid-1941. Capable of carrying a bombload of up to 800kg (1764lbs) externally, the G3M2 was equipped with a defensive armament of three 7.7mm (0.303in) machine-guns in a retractable dorsal turret and two lateral blisters. The new engines gave it a top speed of 374km/h (232mph), with a maximum range of 4380km (2722 miles).

G3M2s first saw combat in August 1937, when the Imperial Japanese Navy examples raided Hangchow and Kwangteh in China.

These raids demonstrated the type's long range, the aircraft flying 2010km (1249 miles) from their base at Taipei in what is now known as Taiwan. By 1940, about 130 examples were serving in China. A year later, further G3M2s were deployed against the Allied forces in the Wake Islands, the Philippines and the Marianas, building up forces in the area in preparation for Japan's entry into the war. On 10 December 1941, only three days after Pearl Harbor, a force of some 60 G3M2s, flying from bases in Indochina, found and sank the two British battleships, HMS *Prince of Wales* and HMS *Repulse,* as they were sailing off the coast of Malaya without fighter escort. This action considerably dented British naval power in the region.

An improved version of the 'Nell', the G3M3 or Model 23, was produced between 1941 and 1943. It was powered by 969.4kW (1300hp) Kinsei 51 radials, which gave the aircraft a top speed of 415km/h (258mph) at 6000m (19,685mph). However, by the second half of the war in the Pacific, the G3M was becoming increasingly outclassed, and examples were deployed in second-line duties from 1943 onwards. It was replaced in service by the G4M. A transport version of the type, converted from the G3M1, was designated the L3Y1 (Model 11), and given the Allied reporting name 'Tina'. Subsequent conversions of G3M2s were likewise designated the L3Y2 (Model 12).

Nakajima B5N 'Kate'

Probably the best torpedo-bomber in service with any air arm when the Japanese entered World War II, the Nakajima B5N had a distinguished war record. Designed by Nakajima, in response to an Imperial Japanese Navy requirement in 1935 to replace the Yokosuka B4Y1, the B5N prototype first flew in January 1937. Fitted with a 596kW (800hp) Nakajima Hikari 2 radial engine, it was a three-seat monoplane with low wings, inward-retracting landing gear for greater stability on landing, and overall a very aerodynamically clean design. Although a prototype was equipped with hydraulically powered flaps and wing folding, the wing-folding version with manually powered flaps was chosen for production. Production aircraft were designated the B5N1, or Navy Type 97 Carrier Attack Bomber Model 1, and they began to be delivered for service on carriers in early 1938, while others were deployed in China. The B5N1 was powered by a 626kW (840hp) Hikari 3 radial. Defensive armament was only one trainable 7.7mm (0.303in) Type 92 machine-gun in the rear cockpit, but it could carry either one 800kg (1764lb) torpedo or an equivalent weight in bombs.

In 1939, an improved variant, the B5N2, was introduced into service, in response to improved fighter aircraft available to the Chinese Nationalist forces. Despite carrying the new 745.7kW (1000hp) Nakajima NK1B Sakae 11 radial engine, it fitted a smaller engine cowling to reduce drag. Armament and bombload were unchanged. The maximum speed of the aircraft rose to 378km/h (235mph) at 3600m (11,811ft). The B5N2 remained in production until 1943, having replaced all the B5N1s in service before the bombing of Pearl Harbor, an attack in which 144 B5N2s were involved. All surviving B5N1s were converted to B5N1-K trainer aircraft. Given the reporting name 'Kate' by the Allies, the B5N2 was responsible for sinking the three American carriers, the USS *Hornet*, USS *Lexington* and USS *Yorktown* in the first year of the war in the Pacific. The type earned the respect of the American forces and would attract the attention of any available defending US fighter during the carrier battles that characterized the fighting in the Pacific. Unfortunately for the Japanese crews, their defensive armament of a single machine-gun, and the type's relatively poor performance, when fully laden with bombs or torpedo, meant that losses began to mount. Although the type figured heavily in the Solomons campaign, it was largely withdrawn after the battles for the Philippines in 1944. Due to their excellent endurance and long range of 1990km (1237 miles), aircraft of this type were then reassigned to anti-submarine and maritime reconnaissance duties in areas beyond the reach of Allied fighters. The anti-submarine aircraft were fitted with magnetic-anomaly detection gear, while the anti-ship aircraft were equipped with radar. Production of all types of B5Ns ended in 1943, having reached a total of 1149 examples.

Specification for B5N2

Country of origin:	Japan
Powerplant:	One 745.7kW (1000hp) Nakajima NK1B Sakae 11 radial piston engine
Armament:	One 7.7mm (0.303in) Type 97 machine-gun, and one 800kg (1764lb) torpedo or equivalent bombload
Weight:	2279kg (5024lbs) empty; 4100kg (9039lbs) loaded
Dimensions:	15.52m (50ft 11in) span; 10.3m (33ft 10in) length; 3.7m (12ft 1in) height; 37.7m² (405.8sq ft) wing area
Performance:	378km/h (235mph) at 3600m (11,811ft); 8260m (27,100ft) ceiling
Flight range:	1990km (1237 miles)
Crew:	Three

AI-317

Aichi D3A 'Val'

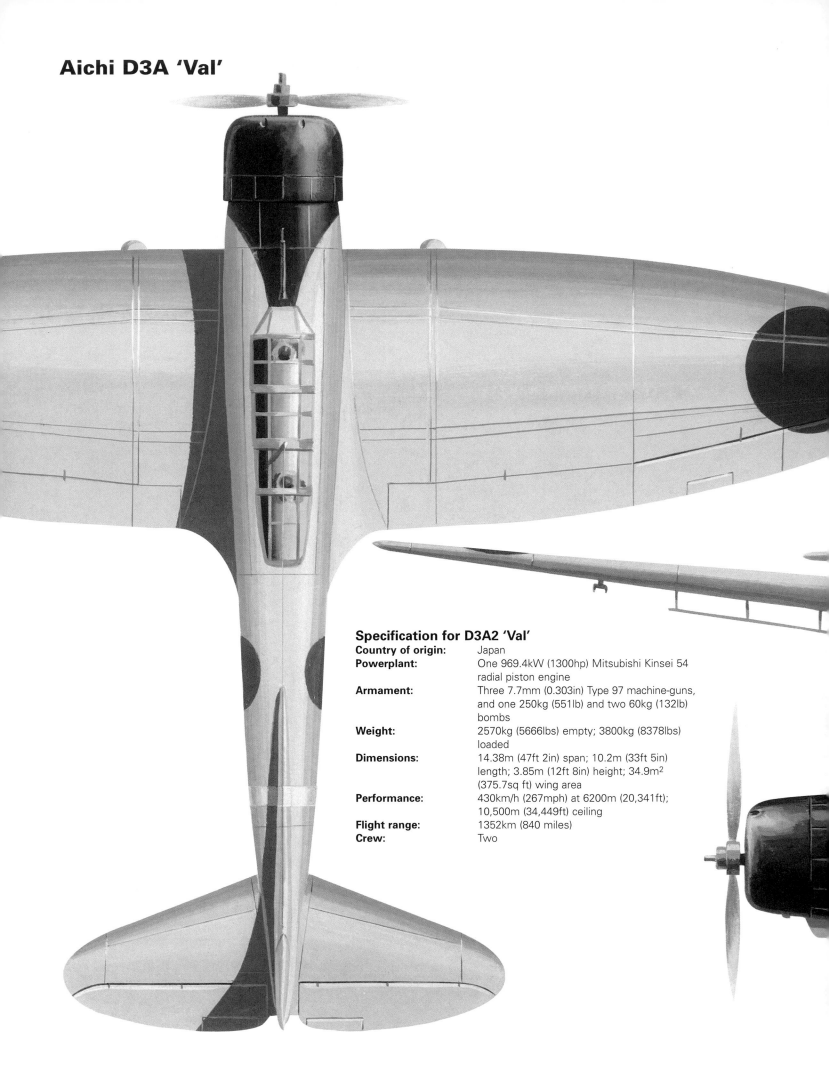

Specification for D3A2 'Val'

Country of origin:	Japan
Powerplant:	One 969.4kW (1300hp) Mitsubishi Kinsei 54 radial piston engine
Armament:	Three 7.7mm (0.303in) Type 97 machine-guns, and one 250kg (551lb) and two 60kg (132lb) bombs
Weight:	2570kg (5666lbs) empty; 3800kg (8378lbs) loaded
Dimensions:	14.38m (47ft 2in) span; 10.2m (33ft 5in) length; 3.85m (12ft 8in) height; 34.9m² (375.7sq ft) wing area
Performance:	430km/h (267mph) at 6200m (20,341ft); 10,500m (34,449ft) ceiling
Flight range:	1352km (840 miles)
Crew:	Two

On the morning of 7 December 1941, it was the Aichi D3A that dropped the first bombs on American targets in Pearl Harbor. In 1936, the Imperial Japanese Navy issued a requirement for a carrier-based dive bomber, and Aichi's prototype first flew in January 1938, powered by a 529.4kW (710hp) Nakajima Hikari I radial engine. Inspired by German aircraft such as the Heinkel He 66, He 70, and He74, the D3A was the first Japanese all-metal, low-wing, monoplane dive-bomber. The second prototype had an increased wing span, strengthened dive brakes and a 626kW (840hp) Mitsubishi Kinsei 3 radial engine. After service trials, the type was put into production as the Navy Type 99 Carrier Bomber Model 11 or Aichi D3A1, now fitted with the 745.7kW (1000hp) Mitsubishi Kinsei 43 radial engine. As a result, it had a maximum speed of 386km/h (240mph) at 3000m (9845ft). The wings were reduced in size from the prototype aircraft, but they retained the fixed, spatted undercarriage. To improve the aircraft's manoeuvrability, a dorsal fin extension from the tailplane was fitted, which gave the D3A1 better handling. The aircraft was fitted with two forward-firing 7.7mm (0.303in) machine-guns, mounted in the nose, and one trainable, rear-facing machine-gun for the navigator.

The type first saw combat as a land-based strike aircraft in China and Indochina, but it was active in the first 10 months of the war as a carrier-based weapon, fighting in all the major carrier actions of that period. It was given the Allied reporting name 'Val'. The D3A1 was responsible for sinking more Allied vessels than any other Axis aircraft during World War II, and was the first carrier-based aircraft in the world to sink a carrier: the British vessel HMS *Hermes*. When used as a dive-bomber, the D3A1 was extremely accurate, due to the high attack angle favoured by Japanese pilots. However, heavy losses encountered both during and after the Battle of the Coral Sea in 1942 led to the D3A1 being withdrawn from carrier duty and transferred to land-based operations.

In response, Aichi produced the D3A2 with an improved engine, the Mitsubishi Kinsei 54 radial, which was capable of providing 969.4kW (1300hp) of power. Fuel capacity was increased to give the type a longer range, and so maximum speed was limited to 430km/h (267mph). Armament remained the two forward-firing, Type 97 machine-guns and one trainable Type 92 in the rear cockpit, while the aircraft had racks to carry one 250kg (551lb) bomb under the centreline and two 60kg (132lb) bombs under the wings.

By 1944, however, the D3A2 was effectively obsolescent, and outclassed by the American fighters in the Pacific. The aircraft served out the rest of the war as a kamikaze aircraft, the pilot sealed into his cockpit in a D3A2 packed with explosives. In total, 476 D3A1 versions and 1016 D3A2s were built.

Mitsubishi A6M2 Model 21 Reisen

Popularly known in Japan as the Zero, this lightweight fighter came as a great shock to the Allies as they reeled under the Japanese onslaught in 1941. It could outmanoeuvre any Allied fighter, and would appear miles from the nearest airbase or carrier. In 1937, Jiro Horikoshi began to design a shipboard fighter that was extremely agile, yet could carry two 20mm (0.79in) cannon and two machine-guns, as well as two 60kg (132lb) bombs, at a speed of 500km/h (311mph), with an endurance of no less than eight hours with a drop tank. The first aircraft flew with the 582kW (780hp) Mitsubishi Zuisei 13 engine, which was not quite quick enough, but the third prototype, the A6M2, was fitted with the 690kW (925hp) Nakajima Sakae 12, which proved to be excellent, and so production was approved in July 1940. They were sent to China for testing, where they shot down 99 aircraft in air combat for no losses, an incredible record that prompted US observers in China to send a warning about the new aircraft to Washington – a warning that was either lost or ignored.

In June 1941, the A6M3 was produced, with clipped wings and a more powerful 843kW (1130hp) Sakae 21 engine, giving it both higher speed and a better roll rate, at the expense of a slight deterioration in turn rate. After the outbreak of war, no Allied fighter could match it, even with lightened armament and reduced ammunition.

On 3 June 1942, however, the Americans captured a Zero intact in the Aleutian Islands, after the pilot broke his neck during a forced landing, and the aircraft's shortcomings were revealed, namely that it achieved such performance at the expense of armour. At the same time new fighters were coming into service, such as the F6F, F4U and P-38, which could hold their own against the fighter, despite being heavier and carrying greater firepower.

The A6M2-N was a seaplane variant that was hampered by its floats and did not achieve much. Horikoshi petitioned to be allowed to build a replacement for the Zero, but was instructed to build an interim aircraft instead, the A6M5, which went on to be the most numerous variant. The main difference was the wing, which was strengthened to improve the aircraft's performance in a dive, while exhaust pipes were positioned to give forward thrust at full power. However, as 1943 progressed, the balance of power in the air swung more and more towards the Allies. Issued in 1944, the A6M5a was a version with a 125-round, belt-fed cannon armament that replaced the 100-round drum. Only weeks later, the A6M5b emerged, with improved armour and fire-extinguishers, and a 13.2mm (0.52in) machine-gun replacing one of the smaller calibre weapons. The A6M6c had an armoured seat, provision for wing-mounted rockets, extra 13.2mm (0.52in) guns in the wing and a larger fuel tank, but no increased power. The A6M7 could carry a 250kg (551lb) bomb. Not until the A6M8 did the type get an improved engine, but this did not fly until May 1945, and did not enter service before the end of the war.

Specification for A6M5b

Country of origin: Japan

Powerplant: One 820.3kW (1100hp) Nakajima NK2f Sakae 12 14-cylinder radial piston engine

Armament: Two 20mm (0.79in) Type 99 cannon with 60 rounds per gun, and two 7.7mm (0.303in) Type 97 machine-guns with 500 rounds per gun, plus two 60kg (132lb) bombs

Weight: 1876kg (4136lbs) empty; 2733kg (6025lbs) loaded

Dimensions: 11m (36ft 1in) span; 9.12m (29ft 11in) length; 3.51m (11ft 6) height; 21.3m² (229.28sq ft) wing area

Performance: 565km/h (351mph) at 6000m (19,685ft); 11,740m (38,517ft) ceiling; 7 minutes to 6000m (19,685ft) climb

Flight range: 1143km (710 miles)

Crew: One

Nakajima Ki-43-II KAI Hayabusa

The Imperial Japanese Army's premier and most modern fighter at the outbreak of World War II, the Nakajima Ki-43 was to prove as big a shock to the complacent Allies in the Far East as the Zero. The prototype was flown in January 1939, after work had first begun on the aircraft in December 1937. The requirement issued by the Japanese Army was for a single-seat fighter armed with two 7.7mm (0.303in) machine-guns, capable of 500km/h (311mph), and a range of 800km (497 miles). The new aircraft was to be as manoeuvrable as the fighter it was intended to replace, the Ki-27.

Nakajima decided to retain the basic wing of the Ki-27, but elongated the fuselage to balance the weight of the 690kW (925hp) Ha-25 radial engine. However, the prototypes were found to be only as fast as the Ki-27, and less manoeuvrable, so a major redesign was initiated, the revised prototypes flying in December 1939. Changes included a more powerful variant of the Ha-25 engine, a lightened fuselage, new vertical tail surfaces, and an improved cockpit. Provision was also made for drop tanks to be carried beneath the wings. A more powerful Ha-105 engine was tested on one of the prototypes, but not used for production aircraft, and a revised armament of two 12.7mm (0.5in) machine-guns was employed on later versions.

What finally persuaded the Japanese Army to adopt it was the use of 'butterfly' combat flaps, which gave the aircraft exceptional manoeuvrability. The Ki-43-I was thus ordered into production as the

Army Type 1 Fighter Model 1, there being three intended subvariants, the I-Ko, I-Otsu, and the I-Hei, which were armed with two 7.7mm (0.303in) guns, one 7.7mm (0.303in) and one 12.7mm (0.5in) gun, and two 12.7mm (0.5in) guns respectively.

The Ki-43 first entered service in June 1941, equipping the 59th Sentai, and was given the name Hayabusa, or peregrine falcon. It was soon to see combat in South-East Asia, where it swept aside the obsolescent Brewster Buffaloes of the Allies, and held its own against the Hurricane IIs hurriedly dispatched to deal with it. However, it was revealed that the wing structures were weak, leading to a number of failures, and redesign work was quickly undertaken. It was also increasingly recognized that the aircraft's performance was lacking and a new engine, the 858kW (1150hp) Nakajima Ha-115, raised the aircraft's speed to 530km/h (329mph) at 4000m (13,125ft). Armour protection was provided for the pilot, as were basic self-sealing tanks. This new aircraft was designated the Ki-43-II, and again there were three versions, the Ko, Otsu and KAI, the latter having revised exhaust stacks that offered some extra thrust.

By late 1942, however, the Ki-43 was struggling against the latest Allied fighters, as manoeuvrability became less important in combat. Nevertheless, it remained in the front line until the end of the war, the last batch being delivered in August 1945. There were two other minor variants, the Ki-43-III-Ko and Otsu, which had uprated engines.

Specification

Country of origin:	Japan
Powerplant:	One 858kW (1150hp) Army Type 1 (Nakajima Ha-115) radial piston engine
Armament:	Two 12.7mm (0.5in) Type 1 (Ho-103) machine-guns, and two 250kg (551b) bombs
Weight:	1910kg (4211lbs) empty; 2925kg (6450lbs) loaded
Dimensions:	10.84m (35ft 7in) span; 8.92m (29ft 3in) length; 3.27m (10ft 9in) height; 21.4m² (230.36sq ft) wing area
Performance:	530km/h (329mph) at 4000m (13,125ft); 11,200m (36,750ft) ceiling; 5 minutes 49 seconds to 5000m (16,405ft) climb
Flight range:	1760km (1094 miles)
Crew:	One

Mitsubishi G4M 'Betty'

Involved in the war from the very beginning, the Mitsubishi G4M remained in service until the end of the war, carrying the Japanese surrender delegation to the ceremony on 19 August 1945. In 1937, the Imperial Japanese Navy issued a requirement for a long-range, medium bomber, and the G4M was the resulting design. The G4M1 prototype first flew on 23 October 1939, and during its service trials demonstrated that it could fly at 444 km/h (276mph), and possessed a range of 5555km (3450 miles), although both these figures were achieved without a bombload. The design was typically Japanese, with a large, glazed nose position for the bomb aimer, and the type was easily recognizable by its dihedral tailplane – in other words the tips of the tailplane were higher than the point where the tailplane was attached to the fuselage.

The aircraft was put into production as the Navy Type 1 Attack Bomber Model 11, and first saw combat against the Chinese in mid-1941. However, the bombers were withdrawn from the theatre shortly before the attack on Malaya, and redeployed to bases in Indochina. Within a week of the invasion, in December 1941, the G4M1 had successfully attacked the British battleships HMS *Repulse* and HMS *Prince of Wales*, which were later sunk. The type was given the Allied reporting name of 'Betty'. It initially proved to be a successful bomber, but following the eventual increase in Allied fighter opposition (both in terms of numbers and quality), the G4M1 proved to be vulnerable. It had very little armour protection for either the fuel tanks or the pilots. In April 1943, the two G4M1s carrying Admiral Yamamoto, one of the most talented Japanese admirals, and his staff were shot down by American P-38 Lightnings over Bougainville.

The Navy Type 1 Attack Bomber Model 22 was little of an improvement, despite its revised powerplant, and so Mitsubishi introduced the G4M2. This variant, powered by 1343kW (1800hp) Mitsubishi Kasei radials, had increased fuel tankage. It also improved the type's defensive armament, with two 7.7mm (0.303in) Type 92 machine-guns in the nose, one Type 92 in each side blister position, and two 20mm Type 99 cannon, one in the tail and one in a dorsal turret. The G4M2 could carry either 1000kg (2205lbs) of bombs, or one 800kg (1764lb) torpedo. Known as the Navy Type 1 Attack Bomber Model 22A or B, the G4M2 remained in production for the remainder of the war, a modified version being designated the Model 24. Although the numbers built declined in the last year or so of the war, a new variant, the G4M3, was produced as the Model 34, with increased crew protection. Only 60 G4M3s were built before the war ended, compared with 1200 G4M1s and 1154 G4M2s. The Yokosuka MXY7 Ohka (the three small artworks below) was a rocket-propelled suicide aircraft with a 1200kg (2646lb) warhead that the G4M could carry under its fuselage.

Specification

Country of origin: Japan

Powerplant: Two 1343kW (1800hp) Mitsubishi MK4P Kasei 21 radial piston engines

Armament: Four 7.7mm (0.303in) Type 92 machine-guns, and two 20mm Type 99 cannon, plus 1000kg (2205lb) bombload or one 800kg (1764lb) bomb

Weight: 8160kg (17,990lbs) empty; 12,500kg (27,558lbs) loaded

Dimensions: 25m (82ft) span; 20m (67ft 7in) length; 6m (19ft 8in) height; 78.13m^2 (840.93sq ft) wing area

Performance: 438km/h (272mph) at 4600m (15,090ft); 8950m (29,365ft) ceiling

Flight range: 6059km (3765 miles)

Crew: Seven

763·12

Specification

Country of origin: Japan

Powerplant: One 880kW (1180hp) Kawasaki Ha-40 V-12 in-line piston engine

Armament: Two 20mm (0.79in) Ho-5 cannon in the nose, and two 12.7mm (0.5in) Type 1 machine-guns in the wings

Weight: 2630kg (5798lbs) empty; 3470kg (7650lbs) loaded

Dimensions: 12m (39ft 4in) span; 8.94m (29ft 4in) length; 3.7m (12ft 2in) height; 20m² (215.3sq ft) wing area

Performance: 590km/h (367mph) at 4260m (13,976ft); 10,000m (32,808ft) ceiling; 7 minutes to 5000m (16,404ft)

Flight range: 1800km (1118 miles)

Crew: One

Unusually for a Japanese fighter, this aircraft was fitted with an in-line engine, which gave it a legacy of problems in service. The connections with German engineering, the leaders in engine technology, began after World War I, when German designers were forced to seek work overseas due to the Treaty of Versailles; as a result, relations developed between the two nations. In the late 1930s, Kawasaki negotiated the rights to build the Daimler-Benz DB 600, and, subsequently, the DB 601. In 1940, the company began to build the 12-cylinder DB601A as the 820kW (1100hp) Ha-40 or Army Type 2 engine. Encouraged by the success of in-line-powered fighters in Europe, Kawasaki proposed a number of such designs to the Imperial Japanese Army; two were selected for further design work. The first was the Ki-60 heavy fighter, and the second, the Ki-61 lighter, all-purpose fighter.

The Ki-61 was based on the Ki-60, with a reduced size fuselage, and an armament of only two nose and two wing-mounted machine-guns. By the time of Pearl Harbor, the prototype was ready, with production lines tooling up. Evaluation of the pre-production aircraft against the P-40, Bf109E-3, Ki-43-II, and Ki-44-I showed its superiority, and Japanese pilots were appreciative of its ability to dive at speed. Production began in late 1942, with two versions: the Ki-61-IA, armed with two 7.7mm (0.303in) and two 12.7mm (0.5in) machine- guns, and the Ki-61-Ib,

with four 12.7mm (0.5in) machine-guns.

Introduced into combat in April 1943, it proved a successful replacement for the Ki-43, largely thanks to its diving speed, but already engine problems were developing; the humid conditions and jungle heat in New Guinea caused stationary aircraft's engines to boil over. Ki-61-Ias and -Ibs were armed with the imported Mauser MG151 cannon in their wings, while the later K-61-KAIc (which appeared in January 1944, and which was the most numerous variant produced that year) had carried four Japanese 20mm (0.79in) cannon. The KAId carried two 30mm (1.2in) cannon in the wings, with two 12.7mm (0.5in) machine-guns in the nose.

An uprated engine, the 1119kW (1500hp) Ha-140, was installed into the Ki-61-II, a prototype of which flew in late 1943. With a larger wing area and improved cockpit, it was ordered into production as the Army Type 3 Fighter Model 2 in September 1944. The KAI version of this airframe was the only Japanese fighter with a heavy enough armament to destroy the B-29, and the performance to reach it at high altitude. After a B-29 raid destroyed the Ha-140 engine factory, KAIs were fitted with radial Mitsubishi Ha-112-II engines. These were rated the best Japanese fighters of the war and designated the Ki-100, but they came too late to turn the tide of the war.

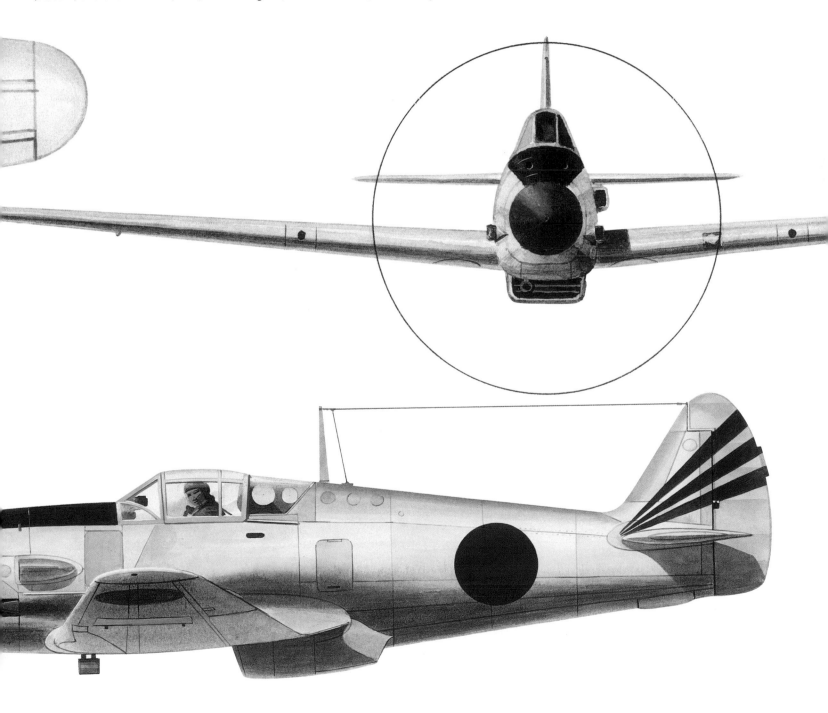

Mitsubishi Ki-67 Hiryu

Designed to replace the Mitsubishi Ki-21 'Sally' and Nakajima Ki-49 'Helen', the Ki-67 Hiryu ('flying dragon') was the best Japanese medium bomber of World War II, but appeared too late to influence the course of the war. Anticipating a future conflict with the Soviet Union in Siberia, Mitsubishi were asked to design a new bomber by the Japanese Air Ministry in November 1940, and Chief Engineer Ozawa began work on the aerodynamic design. Unfortunately for the Japanese, the design process for the Ki-67 was a drawn-out affair, including the very uncharacteristic provision for armour protection and self-sealing tanks. Three prototypes of the Ki-67-I were completed between December 1942 and March 1943, powered by the new double-row Ha-100 18-cylinder radial engines. The first flight took place on 27 December 1942, and the aircraft proved to be fast and manoeuvrable. In fact, unladen, it could perform loops and barrel rolls with ease. It was thus adopted for service as the Army Type 4 Heavy Bomber, capable of carrying 800kg (1765lbs) of bombs – a bombload that would have seen it classified as a medium bomber by the Allies. The production Ki-67-I was fitted with two 1417kW (1900hp) Mitsubishi Ha-104 radial piston engines, giving it a top speed of 537km/h (334mph) at 6000m (19,685ft). Its defensive armament was four 12.7mm (0.5in) Type 1 machine-guns, one each in the nose, tail and beam blisters, with a 20mm (0.79in) Ho-5 cannon in a dorsal turret. However, once more the Japanese Army suggested numerous minor modifications and changes, with the result that production itself was greatly delayed.

However, the Imperial Japanese Navy heard of the type's performance and requested that Mitsubishi convert 100 aircraft to carry the standard 450mm (17.7in) Navy Type 91 Model II aerial torpedo in a rack in the bomb-bay; these entered service in the autumn of 1944. In the meantime, the Army first used its bombers in the summer of 1944, but it was first noticed by the Allies in October, when it was involved in strikes against the US 3rd Fleet, which was attacking Formosa and the Ryukus. The Ki-67 was given the reporting name 'Peggy'. It then appeared over the Philippines, Iwo Jima, Saipan and Tinian, and Okinawa. During the Okinawa campaign, it was also used as a Kamikaze aircraft. In such cases, the aircraft was modified to Ki-67-I KAI standard, which involved removing all armaments and packing a solid nose with explosive.

A new variant, the Ki-67-II, was designed with uprated engines, but only two were ever made. Seriously affected by the Allied bombing campaign against Japan, and a severe earthquake in December 1944, production of the Ki-67-I for both the Japanese Army and Navy amounted to only 696 examples.

Specification

Country of origin:	Japan
Powerplant:	Two 1417kW (1900hp) Army Type 4 (Mitsubishi Ha-104) radial piston engines
Armament:	Four 12.7mm (0.5in) Type 1 machine-guns, and one 20mm (0.79in) Ho-5 cannon, with a 800kg (1765lb) bombload or one Type 91 or Type 94 torpedo
Weight:	8649kg (19,068lbs) empty; 13,765kg (30,346lbs) loaded
Dimensions:	22.5m (73ft 10in) span; 18.7m (61ft 4in) length; 7.7m (25ft 3in) height; 65.85m² (708.86sq ft) wing area
Performance:	537km/h (334mph) at 6000m (19,685ft); 9470m (31,070ft) ceiling
Flight range:	3800km (2360 miles)
Crew:	Six

Polikarpov I-16

Specification

Country of origin: Soviet Union

Powerplant: One 746kW (1000hp) M-62 radial piston engine

Armament: Four 7.62mm (0.3in) ShVAS machine-guns, and a 200kg (441lb) bombload

Weight: 1475kg (3252lbs) empty; 2060kg (4542lbs)

Dimensions: 8.88 m (29ft 2in) span; 6.04m (19ft 10in) length; 2.41m (7ft 11in) height

Performance: 490km/h (304mph) at 3000m (9845ft); 9470m (31.070ft) ceiling

Flight range: 600km (373 miles)

Crew: One

One of the smallest fighters of World War II, the Polikarpov I-16 struggled valiantly against the Luftwaffe after the invasion of Russia in June 1941. At the end of 1931, the Soviet Air Force research institute decided that the future for fighters was monoplane, and ordered the Tupolev design bureau to produce one. The result was the I-14 (or ANT-31) prototype, the most modern fighter in the world at that time. Polikarpov was the designer of one of the then current Soviet fighters, the I-5, and sought permission to design a rival, which flew at the end of 1933. A mixture of fabric, wood and metal went into its construction, but the result was an incredibly short and unstable fighter, less than 6m (20ft) in length, powered by an M-22 engine, a licence-built Jupiter. The prototype's agility and potential won the day, and a Wright Cyclone engine was fitted to the second prototype, which proved to be decisive; the newly designated I-16 was ordered into service.

However, the necessary permission to licence build the Cyclone engine was not yet forthcoming, and the I-16 Type 1 was forced to use the M-22 engine. Deliveries began in late 1934, the Type 1 being armed with two 7.62mm (0.3in) ShKAS machine-guns. By the following year, however, the Type 4 was introduced, with doors to cover the retractable undercarriage, and was powered by the Cyclone engine, a large batch of Wright-built radials having been delivered earlier in 1935. At the same time, the UTI trainer was introduced, fitted with the M-22 engine and two cockpits; later examples had fixed landing gear.

The Type 5 was powered by the M-25, permission finally having been obtained to build the Cyclone engine under that designation. Other modifications included a new propeller, and back armour for the pilot's seat. The 1936 Type 6 mounted an improved 544kW (730hp) M-25A engine. A number were supplied to fight for the Republicans in the Spanish Civil War, outmanoeuvring all the opposition it encountered. Examples survived in Spain until 1950. Various I-16s were supplied to China, where they performed well in the fight against the Japanese, until the A6M Zero appeared in 1940. The Soviet Air Force fought the Japanese directly in 1939, again holding its own against most opposition, although the Ki-27 could out-turn it. The most numerous variant of the I-16 was the Type 10, of which over 2600 were built, fitted with the M-25 engine and an open cockpit, in keeping with the preferences of Soviet pilots.

By the outbreak of the winter war against Finland in late 1939, the main type in service was the I-16 Type 24, powered by a 820kW (1100hp) M63 radial. Although production finished in 1940, lines were reopened in 1941 after the German invasion, despite the obvious fact that the I-16 was no match for the Bf 109F or Fw 190. A number of surviving aircraft were modified to serve as SPB dive-bombers, armed with two 250kg (551lb) bombs, but all types were gradually withdrawn from front-line service by 1943.

Tupolev SB-2

Specification

Country of origin: Soviet Union
Powerplant: Two 619kW (830hp) M-100 V-12 in-line piston engines
Armament: Four 7.62mm (0.3in) ShKAS machine-guns, with a 1000kg (2205lb) bombload
Weight: 5732kg (12,636lbs) loaded
Dimensions: 20.33m (66ft 9in) span; 12.27m (40ft 3in) length; 3.25m (10ft 8in) height; 51.95m² (559.2sq ft) wing area
Performance: 410km/h (255mph) at 4000m (13,125ft); 8500m (27,885ft) ceiling
Flight range: 1200km (746 miles)
Crew: Three

One of the key Soviet light bombers of the 1930s, the Tupolev SB-2 suffered an ignominious fall from grace: once one of the most advanced aircraft in the world, it was relegated to second-line duties in a relatively short space of time, victim of the rapid progress in aircraft design in the mid-to-late 1930s. The ANT-40 prototypes were regarded as being extremely advanced when they first flew in October 1934. A product of Andrei N. Tupolev's design bureau, they were extremely sleek designs for the time, boasting a number of novel features.

As well as being low-slung monoplanes, they were of all-metal construction, and possessed fully enclosed cockpits and retractable landing gear. The aircraft's maximum speed at operating height was no less than 325km/h (202mph), faster than most biplane interceptors then in service around the world. The first prototype was selected as the basis for export versions, and the second was used as the model for the SB-2 bomber that was destined for the Soviet Air Force.

Powered by two 619kW (830hp) M-100 engines – actually licence-built Hispano-Suiza 12Ybrs – the first SB-2s to enter service with the Soviet Air Force in February 1936 were equipped with two-blade, fixed-pitch propellers. Armament was two 7.62mm (0.3in) ShKAS machine-guns in the nose turret, one in a dorsal turret and one more in a ventral position. It could carry a bombload of 1000kg (2205lbs). In October of that year, the SB-2 made its combat debut against the

Nationalist forces in the Spanish Civil War, and eventually some 210 aircraft would serve on the Republican side in that conflict, all manned by Soviet crews. The SB-2 came as a shock to the Nationalist forces, who were all equipped with Heinkel He 51 and FIAT CR.32 biplanes, and they urgently requested better, monoplane fighters. SB-2s were also passed to the Chinese Nationalist forces in their fight against the Japanese, and to Czechoslovakia, where the SB-2 went into licensed production as the B.71 bomber.

The SB-2 performed with some merit until it faced better fighter opposition: first, the Messerschmitt Bf 109 in Spain in 1938 and later, during the Winter War of 1939-40 against Finland, when many of the bombers sent on raids were shot down by the Finns.

As a result, the decision was taken to improve the SB-2, and, as a stopgap, the uprated M-100A engine was installed with variable-pitch propellers. A new variant, the SB-2bis, was built with two 716kW (960hp) M-103 engines and an increased fuel capacity, but armament remained the same. Used as a day bomber, the SB-2 fell in huge numbers after the German invasion in 1941, and it was soon relegated to night-bombing duties.

Other variants included the PS-40 and PS-41 transport versions, and the SB-RK or AR-2, a modified SB-2bis intended for use as a dive-bomber, with a smaller wing area and M-105R supercharged engines.

Petlyanov Pe-2

Often referred to as the Soviet Mosquito, due to its flexibility, the Pe-2 was actually an all-metal design that was built in far greater numbers than its British counterpart. The British first encountered the Pe-2 when two Hurricane fighter squadrons sent to the Soviet Union in 1941 found themselves hard-pressed to keep up with the sleek Soviet bomber. Design on the Pe-2 began when Vladimir M. Petlyanov – best known at this time for his work on the TB-7 (later Pe-8) bomber – was ordered to build a high-altitude fighter, the VI-100. At the time, Petlyanov was in a special prison at GAZ (aircraft factory) No. 156, having been arrested during the extensive Stalinist purges of 1937. Nonetheless, he drew up an extremely modern, stressed-skin design powered by two turbocharged in-line engines. A pilot and radio operator/gunner sat back to back in the main cockpit, separated by a fuel tank. Armament consisted of four 20mm (0.79in) ShVAK cannon in the nose and a 7.62mm (0.3in) machine-gun for the radio operator.

The aircraft first flew sometime in the early summer of 1939, and made its public debut at the 1940 May Day parade. It was able to reach a maximum speed of 630kph (391mph) at 10,000m (32,810ft). However, the Soviet Air Force decided to put the aircraft into production as a three-seat bomber rather than a fighter. A prototype, PB-100, flew in June 1940, equipped with dive brakes, and a redesigned rear fuselage and tail section. The pilot now sat back to back with the navigator/bomb-aimer, who had to squeeze through to his position in the nose of the aircraft during the approach run. The third crew member manned the radio and a lower rear gun. The usual bombload was four FAB-250 (250kg/551lb) or six FAB-100 (100kg/220.5lb) bombs in the main bay. With the latter, two more FAB-100s could be carried in small compartments behind the engine nacelles, or four FAB-100s under the wing roots. The aircraft's armament was changed to two fixed, forward-firing 7.62mm (0.3in) machine-guns, and a machine-gun each for the navigator and radio operator.

The first production aircraft flew in November 1940, powered by 820kW (1100hp) VK-105RA engine, and around 300 were operational by the time of the German invasion the following June. In 1943, the engine was changed to the 940kW (1260hp) VK-105PF/PF-2. Although many variants were built, the main versions produced were the Pe-2 and Pe-2FT bombers, the Pe-2R reconnaissance aircraft, the Pe-2UT trainer, and the Pe-3bis fighter. The Pe-2FT replaced the navigator's machine-gun with a 12.7mm (0.5in) weapon in a lightweight turret. Most of the Pe-3 fighter versions had the bomb-aimer's station removed, and additional guns added to the nose. Sadly, Petlyanov was killed when flying as a passenger in a Pe-2 in January 1942.

Specification

Country of origin:	Soviet Union
Powerplant:	Two 820 (1100hp) Klimov M-105R in-line piston engines
Armament:	One 7.62mm (0.3in) ShKAS, one 12.7mm (0.5in) Beresin UBS, and two 12.7mm (0.5in) Beresin UBT machine-guns, plus up to 1200kg (2646lb) bombload
Weight:	5876kg (12,943lbs) empty; 8496kg (18,730lbs) loaded
Dimensions:	17.16m (56ft 4in) span; 12.66m (41ft 7in) length; 4m (13ft 2in) height; 40.50m² (436sq ft) wing area
Performance:	540km/h (336mph) at 5000m (16,405ft); 8800m (28,870ft) ceiling
Flight range:	1500km (932 miles)
Crew:	Three

Yakovlev Yak 9

The Yak fighter was one of the most numerous types to serve in World War II; over 36,500 were built, and it played a significant part in the defeat of Hitler's Luftwaffe. The first fighter design to emerge from the Yakovlev bureau, the I-26, as the prototype was designated, was built out of a mixture of wood and steel. Powered by the 784kW (1050hp) Klimov M-105 engine, it was armed with one 20mm (0.79in) ShVAK cannon firing through the propeller hub, and two ShKAS 7.62mm (0.3in) machine-guns above the engine. The prototype first flew in January 1940, and as a result the Yak-1 fighter was ordered into production with minor modifications.

However, the Soviet style of manufacture meant that no aircraft was exactly the same, despite the need for standardization and, thus, high output. Modifications made to the design included the replacement of the machine-guns by a single 12.7mm (0.5in) UBS gun in some types, and the field adaptation of cutting away the top of the rear fuselage to improve vision was adopted as the production Yak-1B. The Yak-1M was a significantly better aircraft, featuring the VK-105PF engine and lightened fuselage.

In the meantime, the two-seat trainer version, the Ya-27, had proved to be an excellent aircraft in its own right, largely due to its simplification of the Yak-1 design, and in July 1941, the Yak-7B was produced as a single-seat, fighter version of this aircraft, mostly armed with the 20mm (0.79in) cannon and two UBS machine-guns. A version with an all-metal wing, the Yak-7D, with the cut-down Yak-1B canopy, had more room for fuel, and a range of over 1000km (621 miles). A refined production version of this aircraft became the Yak-9 in mid-1942.

The Yak-9 had a number of improvements, such as redesigned wings, revised rudder and a retractable tailwheel. It carried one 20mm (0.79in) cannon and one or two machine-guns, with provision for rockets under the wings or two bombs. By May 1943, all production had switched to the Yak-9 and its many variants, including anti-tank models armed with guns as big as 57mm (2.25in) and the Yak-9B with capacity for four bombs. The Yak-9U was a further refined variant, with numerous small changes.

In August 1943, a project for an improved dogfighter was revived with the designation Yak-3, featuring a smaller wing and cleaned-up fuselage. It was fitted with the PF-2 engine and proved an immediate success, recognized by both sides as the best dogfighter on the Eastern Front. The Luftwaffe encouraged its pilots to avoid it whenever possible, and it was chosen as the mount of the Free French Normandie-Niemen Regiment, who were offered the pick of any Allied fighter. Like all the Yak aircraft, the Yak-3 had many variants, including a version armed with 57mm (2.25in) guns that only flew once. A two-seater version, the Yak-3UTI trainer, went into service as the Yak-11. A version of the Yak-3, powered by a Soviet copy of the Jumo 004 jet engine, was the first Soviet jet fighter to fly, but this was not until 1946.

Specification for Yak-9U

Country of origin:	Soviet Union
Powerplant:	One 1231kW (1650hp) VK-107A V-12 in-line piston engine
Armament:	One hub-firing, 23mm (0.9in) VYa-23V cannon, and two 12.7mm (0.5in) UBS machine-guns, plus provision for two 100kg (220lb) bombs
Weight:	2575kg (5677lbs) empty; 3098kg (6830lbs) loaded
Dimensions:	9.77m (32ft 1in) span; 8.55m (28ft 1in) length; 2.44m (8ft) height; 17.25m² (185.7sq ft) wing area
Performance:	700km/h (435mph) at 5000m (16,405ft); 11,900m (39,040ft) ceiling
Flight range:	870km (540 miles)
Crew:	One

Mikoyan-Gurevich MiG 1

The first of the MiG fighter line, which was to become so famous after the war, the MiG 1 was a relative failure when introduced to combat. The Mikoyan-Gurevich (MiG) design bureau flew the first prototype, the I-61, in the spring of 1940. Intended to be a high-altitude interceptor, the aircraft was powered by the 895kW (1200hp) Mikulin AM-35 V-12 engine. Following the common Soviet practice of putting a large engine in too small a fuselage, the design suffered handling problems, particularly a lack of stability and pitch problems.

Nevertheless, the I-61, having been redesignated the I-200, was put into production as the MiG 1, with delivery commencing in September 1940. Its handling was not its only fault; the armament of one 12.7mm (0.5in) and two 7.62mm (0.3in) machine-guns would prove to be too light after the invasion of the Soviet Union in 1941, and the aircraft could not absorb much combat damage. Only 100 were built, and these suffered a high proportion of losses in the second half of the year. Nevertheless, as the MiG 1 had a maximum speed of 628km/h (390mph), the Soviet Union boasted that it was the fastest production interceptor in the world in 1940-41.

By that time, the MiG 3 began to arrive with front-line units. Powered by a 1007kW (1350hp) AM-35A engine, with an increased wing dihedral and constant-speed propeller, the MiG 3 had a top speed of 640km/h (398mph), but it proved to be little better than its predecessor. Other modifications included greater fuel capacity, a rear-sliding canopy and larger tyres, but it retained the very short fuselage that caused the handling problems of the MiG 1. It was outflown by both the Messerschmitt Bf 109G and the Focke Wulf Fw 190 at the low and medium altitudes at which most air combat took place, where its heavy engine and poor manoeuvrability put the MiG 3 at an immediate disadvantage. Consequently, it was transferred to attack-bomber escort duties and close-support work.

In 1942, units in the field added two UBX-MG 12.7mm (0.5in) machine-guns in fairings under the wings to increase the type's firepower, but this had the effect of reducing the aircraft's effectiveness. However, the MiG 3 was increasingly outdated, and was gradually replaced by other fighters, such as the La-5 with radial engines that were simpler to maintain. Despite all their flaws, no less than 3322 MiG 3s were built, deliveries ending in 1942 when production of the Am-35A engine ceased. Several attempts were made to produce a better aircraft. The I-210 or MiG-3-82 was equipped with a Shvetsov M-82 radial engine, which was also fitted in the improved I-211 prototype. The MiG 3U reverted to the original AM-35A engine, but none of these entered production.

Specification

Country of origin:	Soviet Union
Powerplant:	One 1007kW (1350hp) Mikulin AM-35A V-12 in-line piston engine
Armament:	One 12.7mm (0.5in) Beresin BS, and two 7.62mm (0.3in) ShKAS nose-mounted machine-guns, plus provision for six 82mm (3.23in) rockets or two 100kg (220lb) bombs
Weight:	2595kg (5721lbs) empty; 3350kg (7385lbs) loaded
Dimensions:	10.3m (33ft 10in) span; 8.15m (26ft 9in) length; 2.67m (8ft 9in) height; 17.44m² (187.7sq ft) wing area
Performance:	640km/h (398mph) at 7000m (22,965ft); 12,000m (39,370ft) ceiling
Flight range:	1250km (777 miles)
Crew:	One

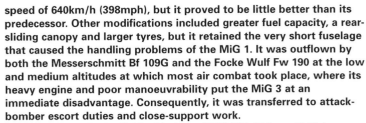

Ilyushin Il-2 'Shturmovik'

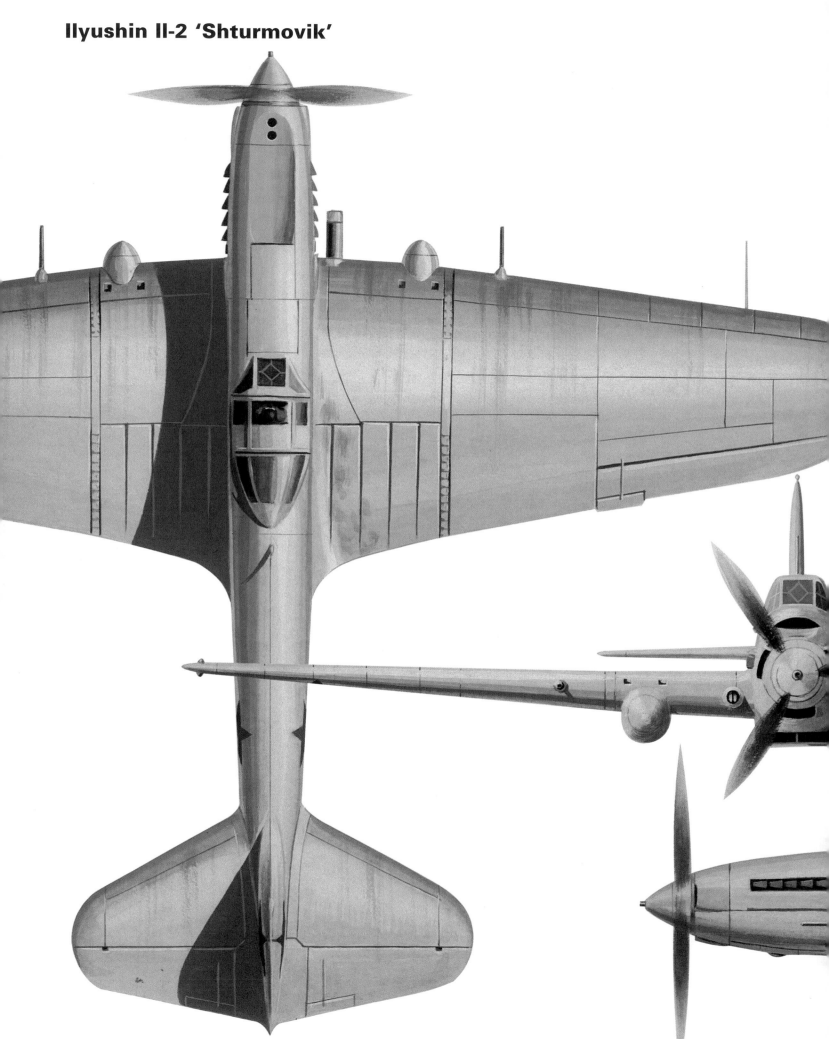

Although it is difficult to say with certainty how many examples of this ubiquitous aircraft were built, Soviet sources put the figure at over 36,000 in total. Intended from the start to be a dedicated, low-altitude, support aircraft, the design was first drawn up as the TsKB-55 in 1938. There were two designs, a single-seat and a two-seat version. The latter encased the engine, radiators, fuel tank and crew in an armoured shell which formed part of the fuselage itself. However, the lighter, single seat TsKB-57 won approval instead. Powered by the 1268kW (1700hp) AM-38 engine, it had a raised, faired canopy for the pilot, two 20mm (0.79in) cannon in place of the four machine-guns mounted on the wing of the two-seat version, and the ability to carry unguided rockets beneath the wings. The first prototype of the TsKB-57 flew in October 1940, and the first production aircraft, with minor modifications to the TsKB-57's design, began reaching front-line units in May 1941, only a month before the German invasion.

Although the Il-2, as the single-seat aircraft had been designated, proved its worth in destroying significant numbers of German armour and transport, many aircraft had been lost, particularly as fighter cover for their operations was not often available in the first desperate year or so on the Eastern Front. It was therefore decided in February 1942 to return to Ilyushin's original two-seat design. To help beat off the Luftwaffe's fighters, the Il-2M – the two-seat aircraft – had provision for a rear gunner under an extended canopy. Two Il-2s were converted to Il-2M status, and, as a result, production aircraft started appearing from September 1942, although some conversions took place in the field.

The Il-2M was fitted with the more powerful AM-38F engine, had increased fuel capacity, and the two 20mm (0.79in) ShVAK cannon were replaced with the more effective 23mm (0.9in) VYa armament. To compensate for the increased armour protection, however, metal panels in its wing were replaced with wooden ones.

The most numerous version produced during World War II was the Il-2M3, or Type 3, which first appeared over Stalingrad in early 1943. It had much better handling than its predecessors, largely due to its redesigned wings, which were swept back 15 degrees on the outer panels.

The Il-2 became increasingly successful as the Soviets developed their tactical methods of employment on the battlefield, and, with increased fighter cover as the war progressed, pilots were able to concentrate on destroying German armour. New weaponry was provided to help them in their task, including cassettes containing 200 hollow-charge, anti-tank bombs and even a DAG-10 anti-aircraft grenade launcher. A few of the Il-2 Type3M variant were produced, mounting a pair of 37mm (1.46in) anti-tank cannon in fairings outboard of the undercarriage, in a manner reminiscent of the 37mm (1.46in) armed Stukas favoured by the Germans.

The Il-2 also saw use by the Soviet Navy, for whom the specialized Il-2T torpedo bomber was developed. The trainer version was designated the Il-2U or U-Il-2, and there was an experimental attempt to fit a radial engine, but this did not go into production.

Specification for Il-2Ms

Country of origin:	Soviet Union
Powerplant:	One 1320kW (1770hp) Mikulin AM 38F in-line piston engine
Armament:	Two 37mm (1.46in) cannon, two 7.62mm (0.3in) ShKAS machine-guns, eight 82mm (3.23in) rockets, and up to 400kg (880lb) bombload
Weight:	4525kg (9976lbs) empty; 6360kg (14,021lbs) loaded
Dimensions:	14.6m (47ft 11in) span, 11.6m (38ft 1in) length; 3.4m (11ft 2in) height; 38.54m^2 (414.4sq ft) wing area
Performance:	404km/h (251mph) at 760m (2500ft); 5945m (19,500ft) ceiling
Flight range:	600km (375 miles)
Crew:	One

Lavochkin La-7

The German invasion of the Soviet Union in June 1941 put enormous pressure on the Soviet Air Force, as the Luftwaffe literally swept it from the skies. One of the fighter types trying to prevent the Germans from gaining air superiority was the LaGG-3, a design from the bureau of Semyon Lavochkin. Although the LaGG-3 was a good fighter by early-war standards, a new type was needed, so Lavochkin began work on a fresh design in October 1941. The LaG-5, as the prototype was known, was powered by the Soviet M-82 radial engine, which was capable of 1194kW (1600hp). A new prototype, with a cut-down rear fuselage to improve visibility, was designated the La-5 and completed its acceptance trials in May 1942. Production began in July, and no less than 1182 examples had been built by the end of the year. The La-5 saw its first large-scale use during the battle for Stalingrad in November 1942.

The following March, the La-5FN began to emerge from the factories, the next major variant of the type. The La-5FN was fitted with the 1231kW (1650hp) ASh-82FN radial engine with direct-fuel injection, which gave it a maximum speed of 647km/h (402mph) at 5000m (16,405ft). It was armed with two nose-mounted 20mm (0.79in) cannon, and could carry either two PTAB anti-tank weapons, two 150kg (331lb) bombs or four 8.2cm (3.23in) rockets mounted under the wing. By 1943, the La-5 was used increasingly in a ground-attack role as well as that of fighter, as it possessed a better performance at both low and medium altitudes, where it could hold its own against the German Focke Wulf Fw190s and Messerschmitt Bf109s. It was used as a fighter-bomber at Kursk, firing hollow-charge weapons at German tanks, before climbing to give support to the Ilyushin Il-2 bombers it accompanied.

Following normal Soviet practice, a two-seat trainer was produced, long after the single-seat fighter had been introduced, as the La-5UTI. Later, La-5s had 23mm (0.9in) cannon to replace the 20mm (0.79in), but in the spring of 1944, a new variant was seen over the Eastern Front: the La-7. Nominally fitted with three 23mm (0.9in) cannon (those built in Moscow only had two), the La-7 had an uprated engine that enabled it to reach the top speed of 680km/h (423mph), along with other minor improvements such as changes in the cockpit outline, and the moving of the oil-cooler intakes. Production of the La-5FN continued, however, and the two types fought side by side. The La-7 was rarely used for ground-attack, but gave cover to the La-5FNs.

The highest-scoring Allied ace of the war, the Soviet pilot Ivan Kozhedub, achieved all his 62 air-combat victories, including a Me 262, while flying either the La-5, La-5FN or La-7, between 26 March 1943 and 19 April 1945.

Specification for La-5FN

Country of origin:	Soviet Union
Powerplant:	One 1231kW (1660hp) ASh-82FN radial piston engine
Armament:	Two 20mm (0.79in) ShVAK cannon, plus provision for four 82mm (3.23in) RS-82 rockets or 150kg (331lb) bombs
Weight:	2605kg (5743lbs) empty; 3360kg (7408lbs) loaded
Dimensions:	9.8m (32ft 2in) span; 8.67m (28ft 5in) length; 2.54m (8ft 4in) height; 17.59m² (189.3sq ft) wing area
Performance:	647km/h (402mph) at 5000m (16,405ft); 11,000m (36,090ft) ceiling
Flight range:	765km (475 miles)
Crew:	One

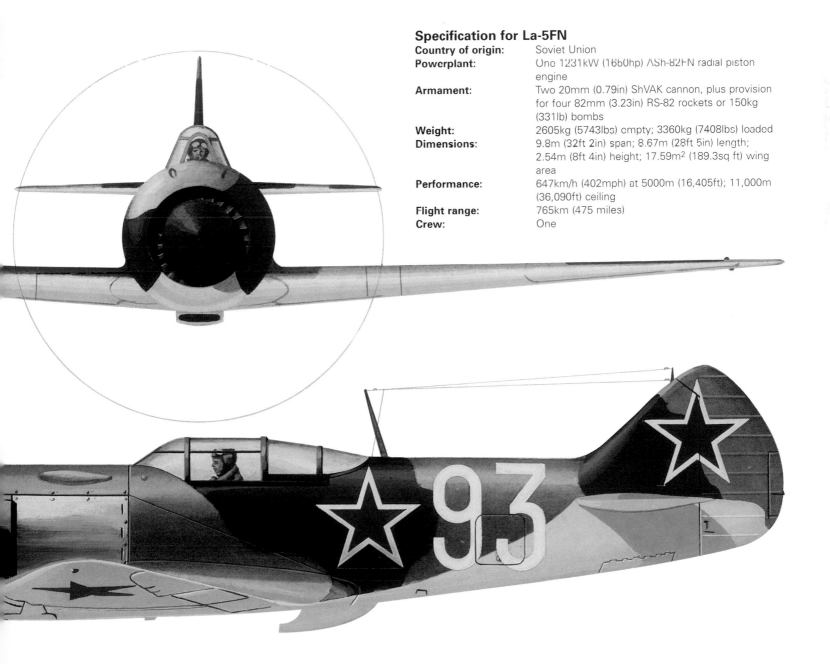

Savoia-Marchetti 79-II 'Sparviero'

Based on a successful airliner, the Savoia-Marchetti S.M.79 was the most successful of Italy's bombers during World War II, taking a heavy toll of Allied shipping in the Mediterranean. The original S.M.79 was a cleaned-up, eight-seat development of the S.M.81, intended for entry in 1934's prestigious 'MacRobertson' race from London to Australia. Although the S.M.79P, powered by three 560kW (750hp) Alfa Romeo 125 RC.35 engines, was not ready in time for that race, it broke numerous speed records the following year. The second prototype was built in 1935 as a bomber, with a bomb-bay offset to starboard, and four defensive machine-guns, one of which was mounted in a pronounced hump on the aircraft's spine, which gave the S.M.79 its nickname of 'il Gobbo', or the 'hunchback'. As a result of the S.M.79P's success, three new versions of the aircraft were launched. The S.M.79T and 79C were both civil aircraft, fitted with the 746kW (1000hp) Piaggio P.XI RC.40 radial engine. Eleven 79Ts were built with extra fuel capacity for transatlantic flights, while the five 79cs were used purely for racing, and both of them continued to break records and win competitions.

The S.M.79B was a twin-engined version, which attracted the interest of several air forces. Iraq and Brazil bought a handful of aircraft, but a major success was achieved with Romania. After buying two batches powered by Gnome-Rhone and Junkers Jumo engines respectively, the Romanians decided to licence-build the S.M.79-JR, which was capable of a top speed of 445km/h (277mph) and later served as a bomber on the Eastern Front.

Production of the Italian Air Force's bomber version, the S.M.79-I, began as early as 1935, entering service the following year and seeing combat in the Spanish Civil War in 1937. At the end of the conflict, 80 S.M.79s were kept by the new Spanish Air Force, remaining in service as a bomber for many years. A variant with uprated engines, the S.M.79-II, with provision for two torpedoes to be carried beneath the fuselage, began to be delivered in 1940. Although the S.M.79 saw service in Africa and Greece, most of its losses were due to its poor serviceability rather than Allied fire. It achieved notable success as an anti-shipping aircraft, however, and sank an number of Royal Navy warships as well as merchantmen.

In late 1943, the final version of the aircraft, the S.M.79-III, was delivered. It had a fixed, 20mm (0.79in) cannon to act as a flak suppressor during a torpedo run instead of the forward-facing, 12.7mm (0.5in) machine-gun. The ventral gondola was also removed, which helped to improve the aircraft's performance, and, to that end, only one torpedo was carried. Increasingly, these S.M.79s, like their earlier counterparts, became unserviceable and by the time of Italy's capitulation, there were only 36 aircraft in an airworthy condition.

Specification

Country of origin:	Italy
Powerplant:	Three 745.7kW (1000hp) Piaggio P XI RC 40 radial piston engines
Armament:	One 7.7mm (0.303in) Lewis, and three 12.7mm (0.5in) Breda-SAFAT machine-guns, plus up to 1250kg (2756lb) bombload or two 450mm (17.7in) torpedoes
Weight:	7600kg (16,755lbs) empty; 11,300kg (24,912lbs) loaded
Dimensions:	21.2m (69ft 7in) span; 16.2m (53ft 2in) length; 4.1m (13ft 6in) height; 61.7m² (664.14sq ft) wing area
Performance:	435km/h (270mph) at 3650m (11,975ft); 7000m (22,966ft) ceiling
Flight range:	2000km (1243 miles)
Crew:	Four

FIAT G.55 'Centauro'

The second low-wing monoplane fighter design from FIAT, the G.55 Centauro was a great improvement on its predecessor, the G.50, but like the majority of Italian designs in World War II, it was not as good as the latest German and Allied aircraft. Designed from the beginning by Giuseppe Gabrielli to be a robust airframe suitable for mass production, the G.55 was nonetheless an aerodynamically advanced aircraft, with smooth contours and the raised cockpit set well back, close to the centre of gravity.

The first prototype flew on 30 April 1942, and the design proved itself to be fast and manoeuvrable, and thus was popular with its pilots. The third prototype was the first to be armed, carrying one 20mm (0.79in) Mauser MG 151/20 cannon in the engine (firing through the propeller hub), and four fuselage-mounted machine-guns. However, on the production aircraft, the armament was changed to three cannon, two mounted on the wing as well as the original one in the engine, and two fuselage-mounted, 12.7mm (0.5in) Breda-SAFAT machine-guns. Provision was also made to carry two 160kg (353lb) bombs on racks under the wings. To carry this weight, the G.55 was powered by a 1100kW (1475hp) FIAT RA 1050 RC-58 Tifone (actually a licence-built Daimler-Benz DB 605A) in-line engine, which gave it a maximum speed of 630km/h (391mph).

From March 1943, the G.55 was evaluated under operational conditions, but the Italian Air Ministry had already decided to go ahead with production and awarded a contract with FIAT for the type. Sixteen G.55/0 pre-production aircraft were built before the first G.55/1 production examples emerged from the factory. However, only 15 G.55/1s were completed before Mussolini was overthrown and Italy went over to the Allies; they served with the Regia Aeronautica (the Italian Air Force) in the defence of Rome. Subsequent examples were built for the Fascist air arm that continued to fight alongside the Luftwaffe, most of which were based near Venice. Total production was 274 before the end of the war. Although losses increased as the war came to an end, this was largely due to the Allied bombing campaign, and the type continued to perform reasonably well in the air.

The G.56 was a prototype built in early 1944 and fitted with a more powerful engine, the Daimler-Benz DB 603A. Two examples were made, incorporating minor structural changes – largely to allow for the new engine – and the deletion of the two fuselage-mounted machine-guns. However, the decision was made not to proceed, although one G.56 survived to become a testbed for FIAT.

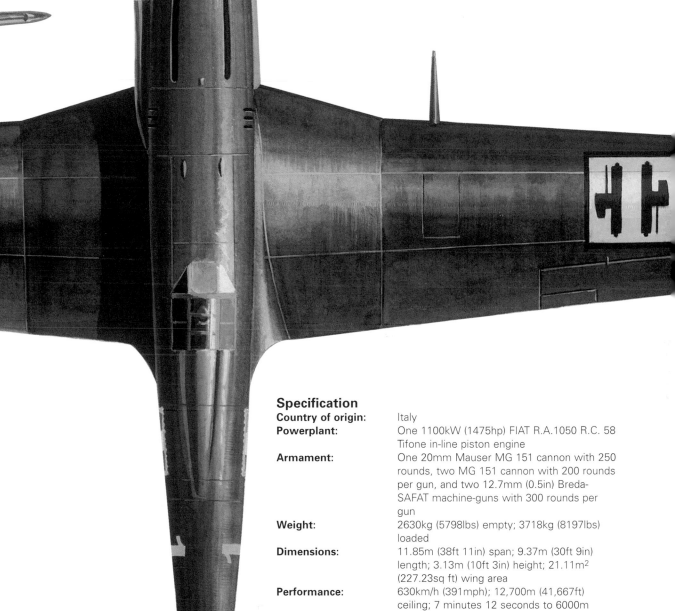

Specification

Country of origin:	Italy
Powerplant:	One 1100kW (1475hp) FIAT R.A.1050 R.C. 58 Tifone in-line piston engine
Armament:	One 20mm Mauser MG 151 cannon with 250 rounds, two MG 151 cannon with 200 rounds per gun, and two 12.7mm (0.5in) Breda-SAFAT machine-guns with 300 rounds per gun
Weight:	2630kg (5798lbs) empty; 3718kg (8197lbs) loaded
Dimensions:	11.85m (38ft 11in) span; 9.37m (30ft 9in) length; 3.13m (10ft 3in) height; 21.11m² (227.23sq ft) wing area
Performance:	630km/h (391mph); 12,700m (41,667ft) ceiling; 7 minutes 12 seconds to 6000m (19,685ft)
Flight range:	1200km (746 miles)
Crew:	One

Dewoitine D.520

Specification

Country of origin: France

Powerplant: One 697kW (935mph) Hispano-Suiza 12Y 45 in-line piston engine

Armament: One 20mm (0.79in) HS 404 cannon, and four 7.5mm (0.295in) MAC 34 M39 machine-guns

Weight: 2036kg (4489lbs) empty; 2677kg (5902lbs) loaded

Dimensions: 10.2m (33ft 6in) span; 8.6m (28ft 3in) length; 2.57m (8ft 5in) height; 15.97m² (171.91sq ft) wing span

Performance: 534km/h (332mph) at 5500m (18,045ft); 10500m (34,450ft) ceiling

Flight range: 1530km (950 miles)

Crew: One

The French equivalent of the Hawker Hurricane, the Dewoitine D.520 was inferior to the Messerschmitt Bf109E, but fought with great determination during the Battle for France. Built in response to a French Air Ministry requirement of July 1934 for a new interceptor, work on the project did not begin until June 1936, when Robert Castello was instructed to start work on a fighter to be powered by the Hispano-Suiza 12Y-21 engine and capable of 500km/h (311mph). The French Air Ministry demanded a minimum of 520km/h (323mph), which resulted in a redesign of the aircraft now designated the D.520. The wings were shortened and a new 895kW (1200hp) Hispano-Suiza engine proposed. Although this too was rejected, Dewoitine persevered, and by the time a privately funded prototype was nearing completion, the air ministry awarded a contract for the aircraft.

The first flight was made on 2 October 1938 using an early engine design, but once this was replaced with a Hispano-Suiza 12Y-29 engine, and the twin radiators were replaced with a single, central one, the prototype met its speed requirements. A second prototype, with a redesigned tail unit, flew in January 1939, armed with an engine-mounted, 20mm (0.79in) cannon and two machine-guns under the wings.

On 17 April 1939, an order for 200 D.520s was placed by the Air Ministry, conditional on delivery being completed by the end of the year. Looming war clouds meant that further contracts were placed in June and September 1939, and January, April and May 1940, a total of 2200 aircraft. However, not one production example had flown by the time war broke out in September 1939, and only 13 aircraft had been completed by 1 January 1940. By the time of the German invasion in May 1940, only 36 D.520s were operational. The type's first combat experience came on 13 May, when it shot down three Henschel Hs 126s and a Heinkel He 111 without loss. The following day, it encountered Bf 109s for the first time, and suffered its first losses. It achieved some success against the Luftwaffe, and fared better against the Italian Air Force when it joined the war on 10 June. The first examples reached the French Navy in June, but none saw combat before the armistice was signed.

After the armistice, many of the D.520s served with the Vichy Air Force in North Africa, and also saw action against the Fleet Air Arm in Syria. In April 1941, the Germans permitted the production of D.520s to continue, which saw 349 completed by the end of 1942, 197 of which were powered by the Hispano-Suiza 12Y-49 engine. Many were involved in the Vichy defence of North Africa after Operation Torch, the Allied landings in November 1942. After this, most of the French pilots joined the Allies, and the Vichy Air Force was demobilized by the Germans when they occupied southern France. The surviving D.520s were used by the German, Italian, Romanian and Bulgarian Air Forces on the Eastern Front, and latterly, for training. A number of D.520s also served with the Free French Air Force after the invasion of southern France.

PZL P11

Specification

Country of origin: Poland

Powerplant: One 481kW (645hp) P.Z.L.-built Bristol Mercury VI.S2 radial piston engine

Armament: Two 7.7mm (0.303in) machine guns, plus underwing racks for lightweight bombs

Weight: 1147kg (2529lbs) empty; 1630kg (3594lbs) loaded

Dimensions: 10.72m (35ft 2in) span; 7.55m (24ft 9in) length; 2.85m (9ft 4in) height; 17.9m² (192.68sq ft) wing area

Performance: 390km/h (242mph) at 5500m (18,045ft); 8000m (26,245ft) ceiling

Flight range: 700km (435 miles)

Crew: One

When Germany invaded Poland in September 1939, the PZL P.11 equipped 12 squadrons; although the country was quickly overrun, this small, outdated fighter would claim to have shot down 126 Luftwaffe aircraft for the loss of 114 of their own. Although in theory no match for the latest German types, the skilled Polish pilots proved adept at air combat, something they would later show again whilst serving with the RAF in the Battle of Britain.

The design of the P.11 can be traced back to the prototype PZL P.1 fighter, which was the first to fly with Zygmunt Pulawski's unique wing. To give pilots the best possible view, he used the 'gull-wing' shape to build a high-wing monoplane. Although the prototypes were flown with Hispano-Suiza engines, a deal had been struck with the English engine manufacturer Bristol to licence-build the Jupiter radial, and so PZL built four more prototypes, the first flying in August 1930. The P.6/I was fitted with the low-altitude 336kW (459hp) Jupiter VI, whilst the P.7/I was powered by the high-altitude 363kW (485hp) Jupiter VII. The P.6/II had a revised exhaust system, and the P.7/II had a redesigned rear fuselage structure. This latter design entered service with the Polish Air Force in late 1932 as the P.7a, which meant that in late 1933 Poland was the first country in the world to have a front-line force of all-metal, monoplane fighters. Approximately 100 were still in service in 1939.

The use of the Jupiter radial engine had spoilt the excellent view for the pilot in the initial prototype, and so it was suggested that the airframe might be fitted with a smaller radial, namely the Bristol Mercury, a variant that would be designated the PZL P.11. However, a delay in the Mercury engine arriving saw the prototype P.11/I being flown with a 384kW (515hp) Jupiter IX.ASb. Only in December 1931 would the P.11/II prototype fly with a Mercury IVa engine. A third prototype served as the pre-production model, which was accepted into service as the P.11a, although some 50 P.11b aircraft powered by Gnome-Rhone Mistral engines had already entered service with Romania. The P.11a was fitted with the Skoda-built Mercury IV.S2 engines, which could deliver 386kW (517hp).

The major production variant was the P.11c, which, to improve the pilot's view further, moved the engine downwards and raised the pilot's seat, moving it backwards at the same time. The first batch of 175 examples were powered by the 418kW (560hp) Mercury V.S2, and the remainder by the VI.S2. IAR of Romania built about 80 examples of the P.11c fitted with the 9K Mistral engine, which was designated the P.11f. Deliveries to the Polish Air Force finished in 1936, but the outbreak of war saw the P.11g designed, using the Mercury VIIIa engine, with a four-gun armament. However, the country was occupied before production could begin. Finally, an export version with Gnome-Rhone engines, designated the P.24, served with Turkey, Bulgaria, Romania and Greece.